AF262576

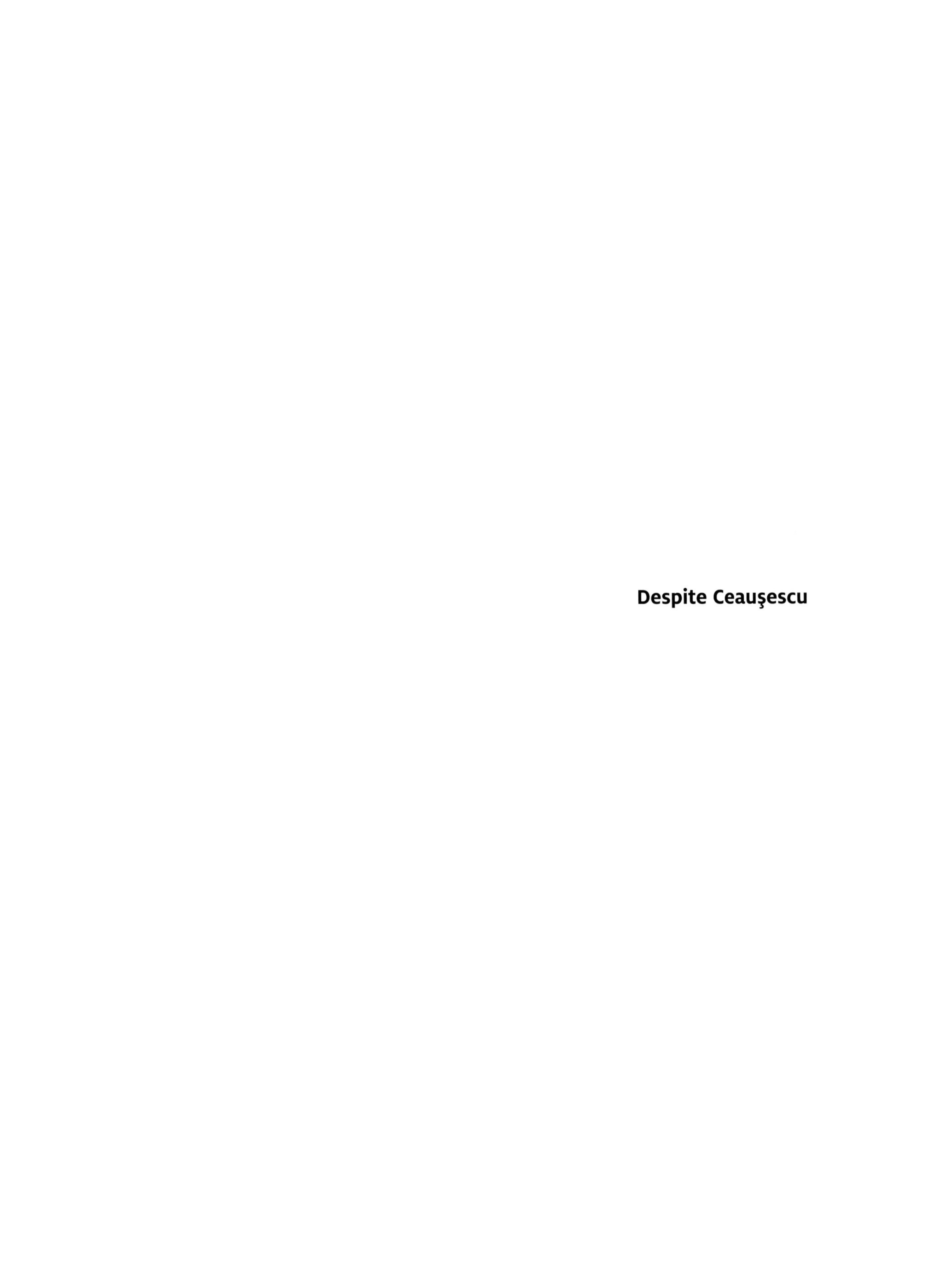

Despite Ceauşescu

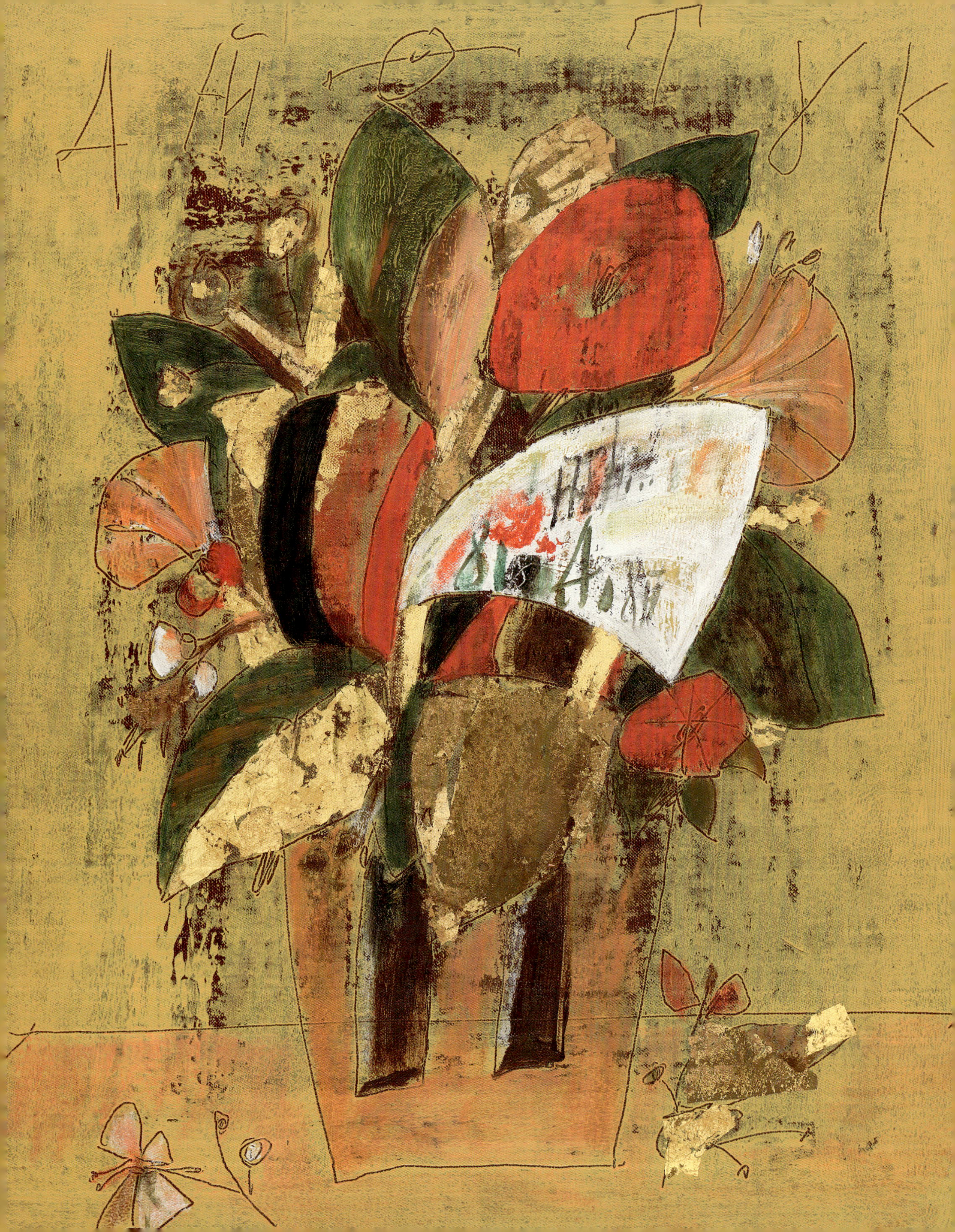

Frances Tyler   **Despite Ceauşescu** : A Collection of Romanian Art

Published in Washington, DC, USA,
by the author.
© Frances Stevenson Tyler, 2021.
All rights reserved.

Library of Congress Control Number:
2021910853
ISBN: 978-0-578-92460-1

All photography is by Lee Ewing except
for *Composition* on page 11, by Rachael Rose

Opposite: Vasile Gorduz, *Ordinary Bird
(Bird Sleeping)* (cat. 6)

Cover: Corneliu Petrescu, *Untitled* (detail,
cat. 39); frontispiece: Corneliu Petrescu,
Flowers (detail, cat. 47); page 8: Corneliu
Petrescu, *End of Winter* (detail, cat. 29);
page 72: Corneliu Petrescu, *Untitled* (detail,
cat. 52); page 92: Silvia Radu, *Bowl with
Stand* (detail, cat. 75)

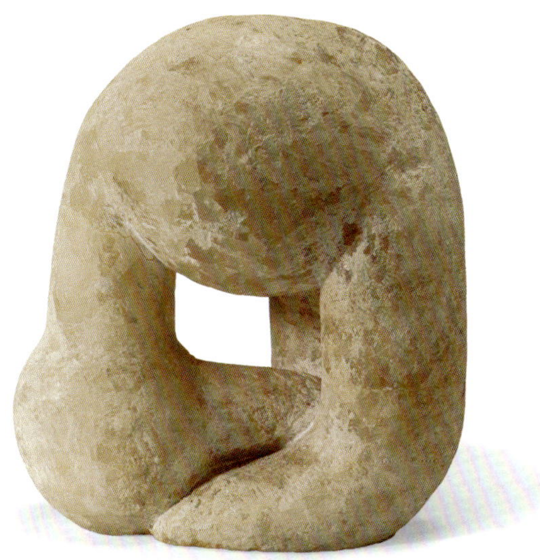

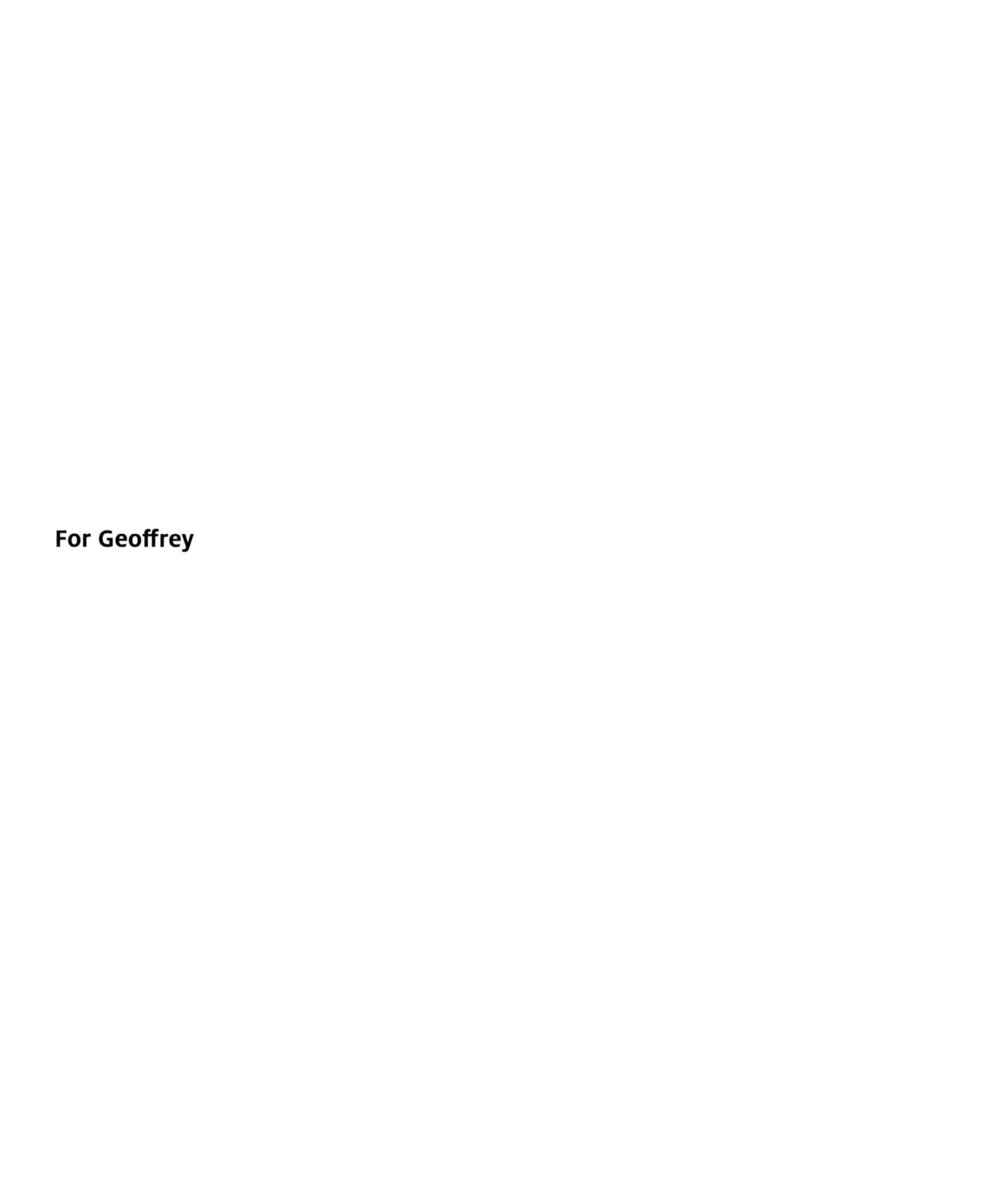

For Geoffrey

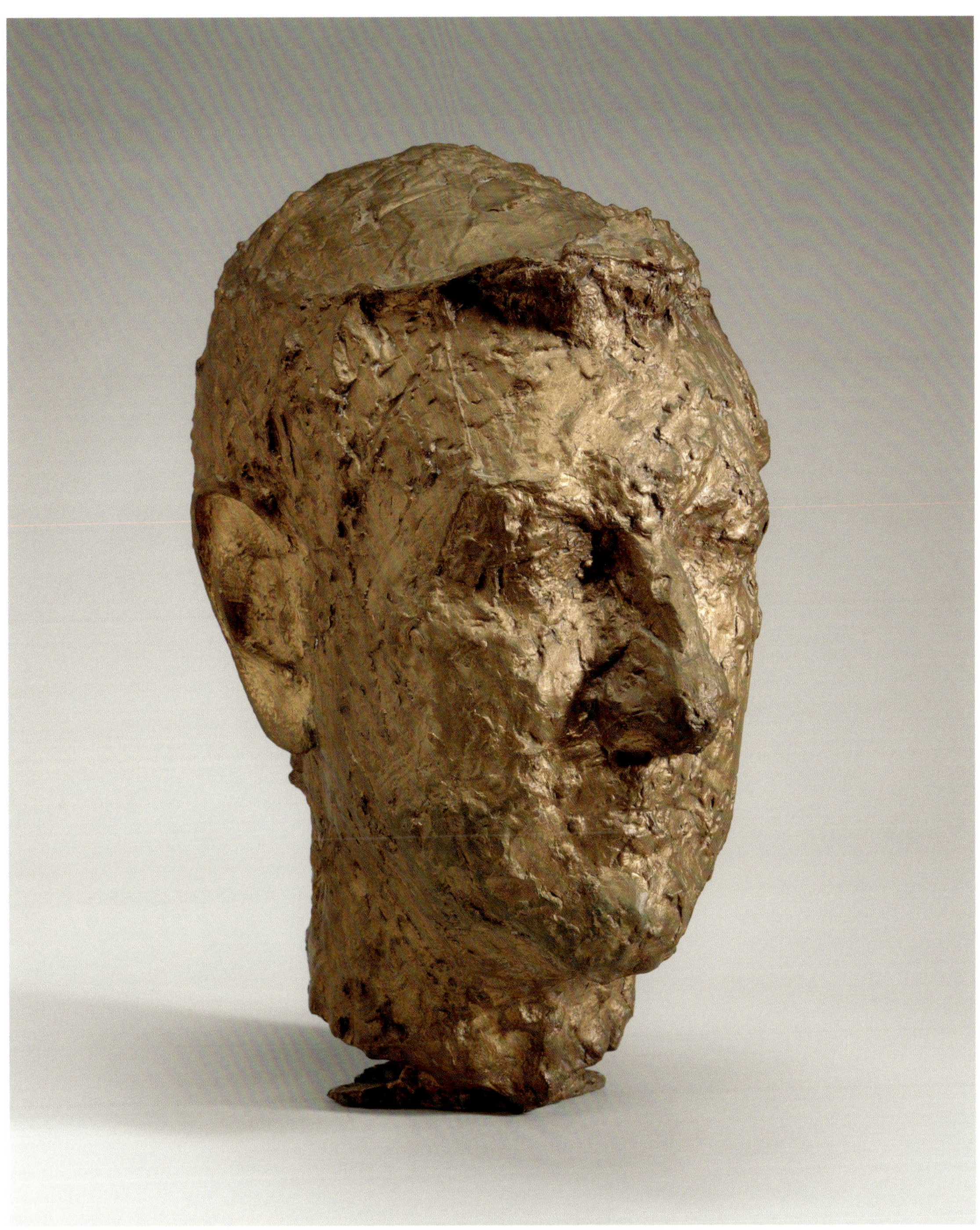

Vasile Gorduz, *Portrait of Geoffrey Tyler*, undated, bronze (cat. 7)

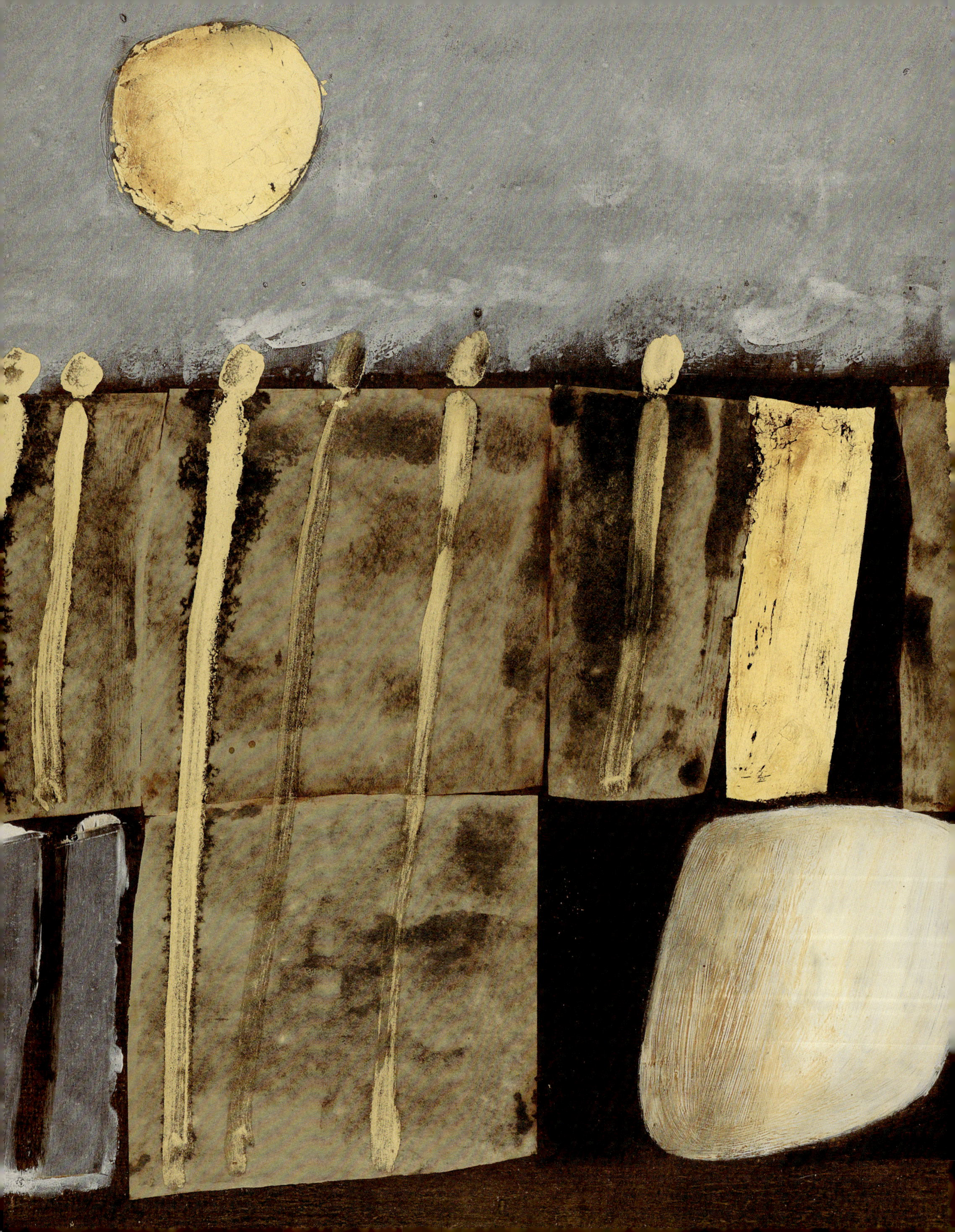

Preface

"A small miracle," Geoffrey called it — Geoffrey Tyler, my late husband, and the hero of this story. He would recall the event again and again in his correspondence over the years with the artist Corneliu Petrescu and his wife Mariana, a frequent and lively correspondence, over four decades to the end of his life, which sustained all of them — and which stirs up my own memories as I write this.

Geoffrey had spotted a painting in the window of an art gallery: this was Fondul Plastic, the state-run art gallery in Bucharest. The year was 1973. Geoffrey was there to represent the International Monetary Fund in negotiations with the Romanian Ministry of Finance. He was just then taking a break from talks and, as he tells it, "was working in my room at the Intercontinental and just felt that I wanted some fresh air and a little exercise and turned right at the entrance of the hotel, crossed the street, took a look at the nice old church that Ceausescu later destroyed, and then reached Fondul Plastic."[1]

It wasn't just art that interested Geoffrey. He was a man of many parts and more than an amateur. With rigor and finesse he immersed himself in jazz and classical music; in buying Turkish and Persian rugs and English antique silver with a discerning eye; and amassing a huge collection of cookbooks from all over the world to produce fine cuisine. He enjoyed tennis, basketball, and squash; cars (Corvettes and Mercedes); and women, undoubtedly (I was his last of several wives). He was fond of cats.

Geoffrey rose through the ranks of the IMF, becoming Assistant Director of the European Department; I picture him as a demanding but fair boss. It had not been a straight path from his native

Australia. Growing up in Melbourne and Hobart, Tasmania, he studied meteorology at the University of Tasmania and moved to Melbourne to become a TV meteorologist. Soon he decided on a new direction, and earned a master's degree in economics at the University of Melbourne. Completing this with distinction, he served as an economist with the Australian Treasury in Canberra, and from there he was recruited to the IMF.

Geoffrey was proud of being a very fast walker, and so it is all the more surprising that he paused long enough, with his colleague, Alison Mitchell, to notice a work of art. "Although it was I who went into the shop to buy the painting, there was another one in a folder. Both were unframed apart from a matt. The one in the window was what I would call a 'door' in basically an overall brown looking design in [the artist's] 'Klee' style. The one inside Fondul Plastic was from the 'Memories of a Museum' series, based on primitive Italian paintings of the 12–13th centuries. At the time I preferred it, but so too did Alison, who decided to buy one also. In gentlemanly fashion I gave her first choice and I bought the 'door' that was in the window."[2] Geoffrey later found a similar "Memories" example for himself. A collector was born.

Back in Washington a year later, Alison "went to the trouble, knowing that 'our artist' was in the U.S., of ringing the Romanian Embassy to enquire about his whereabouts and to arrange with him to meet us on Independence Day." So it was that Geoffrey first met Corneliu Petrescu. Geoffrey and his wife Maria "took him, together with Alison Mitchell to Charles Baker's barbeque"— two extra guests

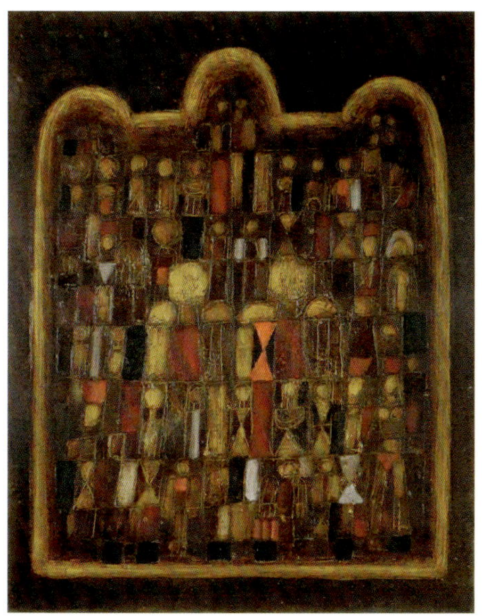

Corneliu Petrescu, *Composition*, 1972, mixed media on paper. Tyler Collection of Romanian and Modern Art, University of Tasmania (UTT 2013/126). More than likely, this is the work that Geoffrey purchased at Fondul Plastic in 1973.

for their friend but reluctant host. "However, Maria bullied him into having you both. And in fairness to him, he was very hospitable and, I think, pleased to be able to introduce an artist from Europe to his other guests."[3] Geoffrey and Maria had promised to eat less steak and potatoes.

The annual IMF mission to Romania usually happened in the late spring or early summer, and in May 1975, Geoffrey dined with the Petrescus either at their apartment on Strada Dimitrie Marinescu or at a restaurant downstairs. Here, to celebrate their new friendship, Corneliu gave Geoffrey his self-portrait and one of Mariana (see pages 12–13).

This friendship became the mainstay of all their lives. Decades later, following Corneliu's death on May 3, 2009, Geoffrey wrote letters of condolence to Mariana almost daily. In one, he recalled Corneliu's generosity in introducing him to his artist colleagues: "Obviously there were the Gorduz.... he also introduced me to [Ion] Pacea, [Gheorghe] Saru and [Ion] Gheorghiu amongst others and enabled me to add their works to my collection." Corneliu took great trouble "to find Romanian paintings to add to my collection in order to make it as representative as possible."[4]

Corneliu — truly the second hero of this story — was self-trained as an artist and well versed in art history, although he had first pursued a medical career. Mariana wholeheartedly supported him in his gifts so that he could develop "a personal style that was unique and that served him wonderfully in producing the paintings that expressed his view of the world."[5] Geoffrey's own pleasure in visiting museums owed much to Corneliu, he wrote to Mariana. "He had such a wonderful eye for

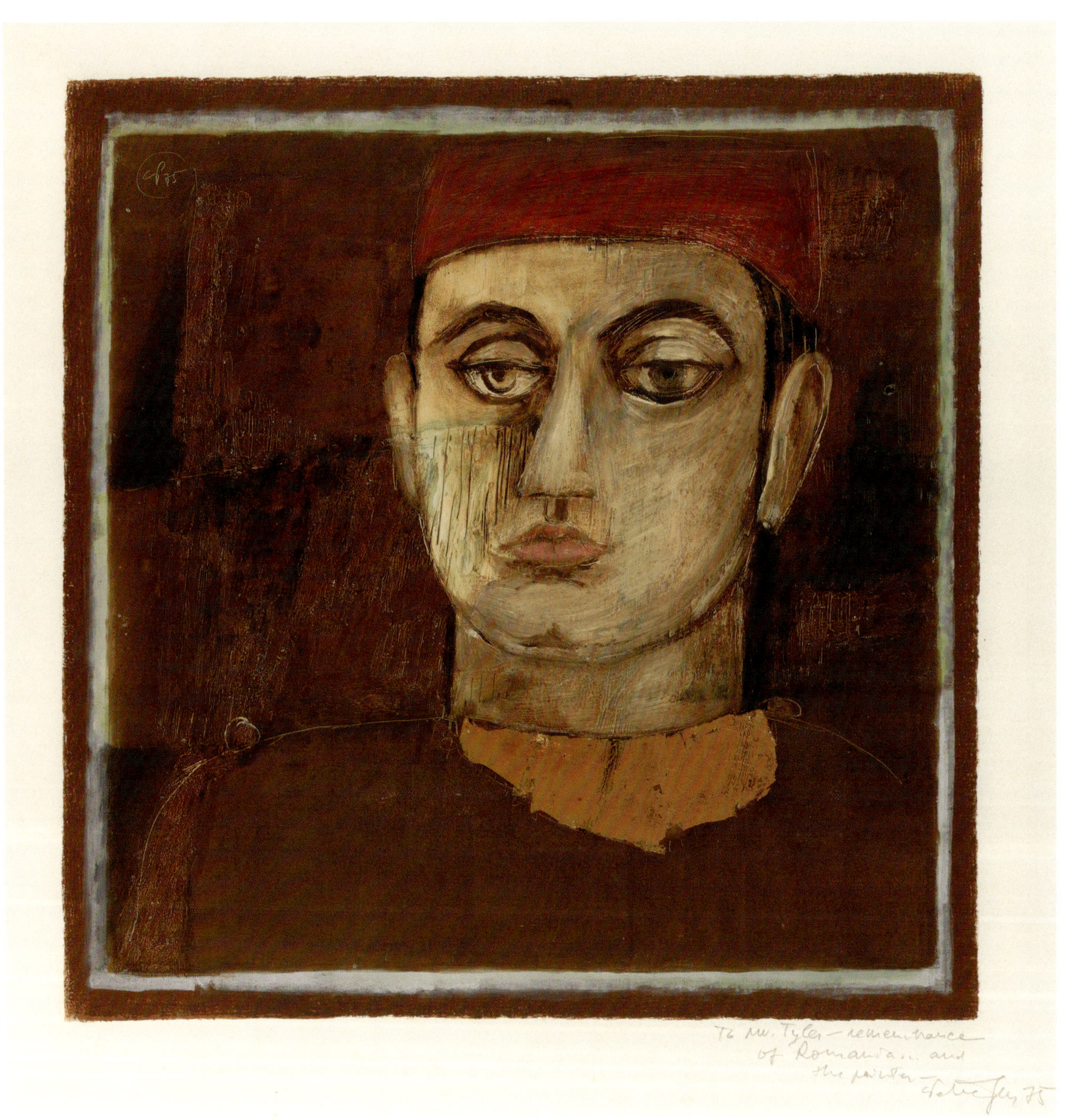

Corneliu Petrescu, *Self-Portrait*, 1975, oil on paper (cat. 22)

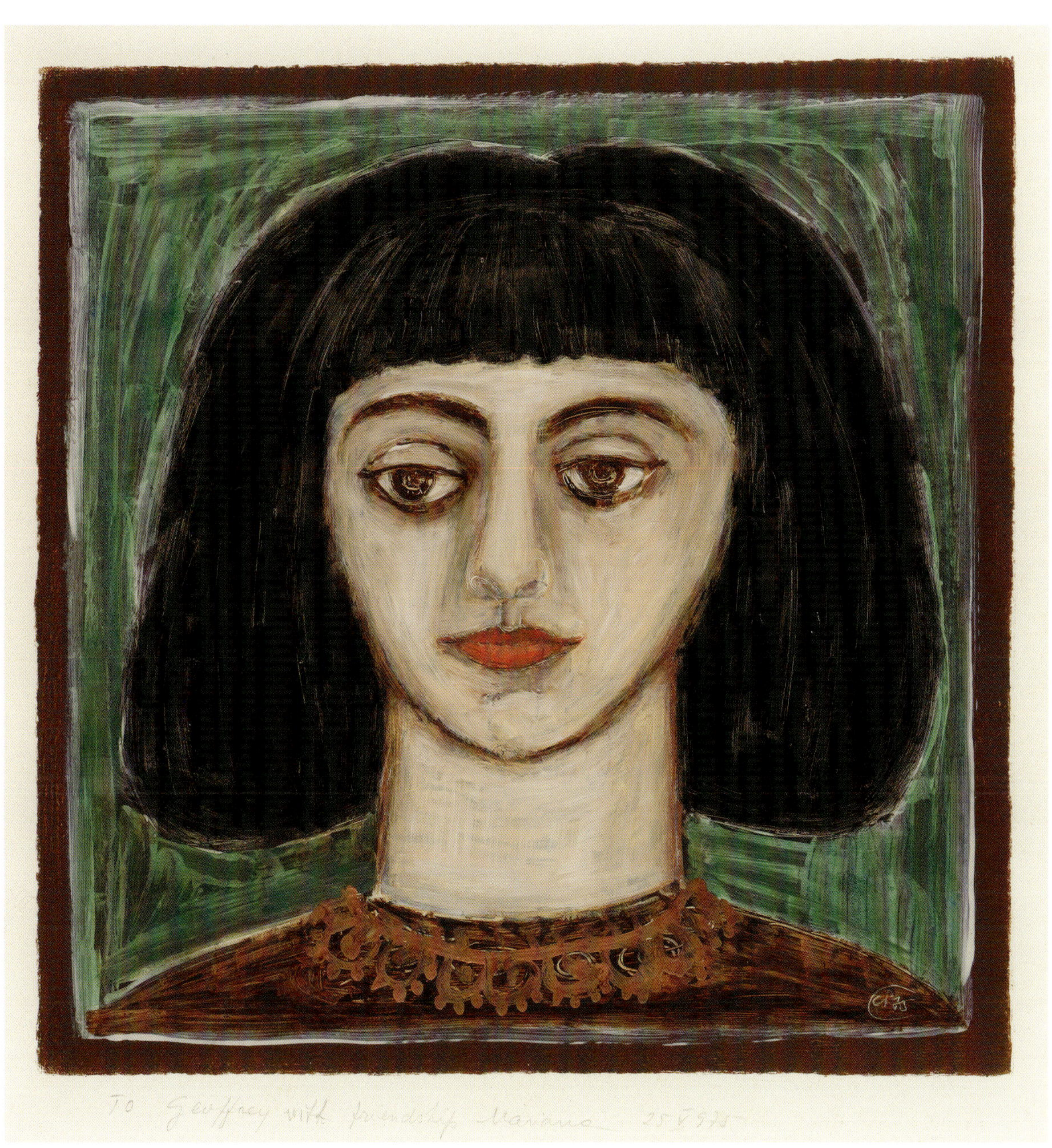

Corneliu Petrescu, *Mariana*, 1975, oil on paper (cat. 23)

paintings, in terms of who had painted them, the techniques used and where the beauty lay. It was a wonderful gift that he gave to me over the years to be able to visit unknown museums and see new things, with an understanding of the way in which an artist thinks about his work. . . . By some chance, we thought of many things the same way and were able to jointly share things even though we came from such different countries and backgrounds."[6]

Geoffrey's other important friendship in Romania was with Vasile Gorduz and Silvia Radu, who were husband and wife. This was despite a language barrier — neither of them knew English, although both Geoffrey and Silvia knew a little French. He wrote to them, "It was a very lucky day for me when Corneliu took me to 29B [Strada Ermil Pangrati] and introduced us. . . . I was given not only friendship but an introduction to the life of artists and their works that few non-artists can have" and "which cannot be learnt from books and museums." Geoffrey believed that "few people own sculpture," because it "is expensive and less easy to comprehend" than paintings.[7] Nevertheless, "My house is full of works of Radu/Gorduz and whatever room I am in there is something to remind me of you both — porcelains, including heads, bronzes, carved stone, paintings or icons that you gave me or helped me obtain." It was not only the love of sculpture that the Gorduz gave to him, "but also the knowledge and love of painting from icons on wood and glass."[8]

In 1981, Silvia gave Geoffrey her gilded bronze relief, *Dacian Warriors*. "That work had an adventure on its way to Washington," Geoffrey told her and Vasile. "I did not return to the U.S. directly, since I had to go to a mission in Poland. It was late in 1981, if I remember the date correctly. The relief was wrapped in a Romanian blanket that you, Vasile, used to wrap around your waist for warmth. I could not fit it in my suitcase and therefore had to carry it as an extra piece of hand luggage. It was heavy. In Warsaw, the military coup took place while I was there. All travel into and from Poland was stopped and the Fund mission was finally able to leave only by special permission, at very short notice, by train to Prague. I remember having to board the train in Warsaw at the very last minute before it left. In fact I almost fell off climbing up the moving steps carrying the relief under one arm. The relief thus had a voyage to Poland, via Germany, another to Czechoslovakia, then to France to finally caught [sic] a plane to the U.S."[9]

The typical IMF mission was very hard work, after equally arduous preparation in Washington. Geoffrey's packing, also, included a list for the Petrescus —"gold leaf, rubber gloves, etc. to bring with me, not forgetting Kent cigarettes"— and denim jeans and Beatles tapes.[10] On these missions "one is stuck together with a group of people, some of whom one has nothing in common [with] except work. One works with them, eats with them and lives with them for several weeks, in hotels and meeting rooms. Fortunately I enjoyed the work of a mission." Moreover, thanks to the Petrescus and their artist friends, "I had evenings and days in the company of you and Corneliu, eating genuine Romanian food in a genuine Romanian apartment. Meeting genuine Romanian people.... This turned a Romanian mission from what could have been almost a hardship into what was almost a vacation."[11]

Geoffrey was not the only one on a mission to be drawn to the artworks. His colleagues also saw the unique chance to buy from artists whose work, during Nicolae Ceaușescu's oppressive rule (1965–89), could not be found outside Romania. Geoffrey touted "the overall quality of Romanian painters in the second half of the 20th century. The technique and ability of the artists to put their thoughts onto canvas and the quality of those thoughts were very high indeed."[12] Elsewhere he added, "It is to the credit of the artists that they had to work in the political environment of a closed Communist controlled society that puts limits on artists lives, for example the freedom to travel abroad."[13] Fortunately, "Corneliu sold quite a number of paintings to mission members at prices that were reasonable to him and the buyer and the same was true to a smaller extent for Silvia, who sold quite a few ceramics"— not to mention "the additional point that the buyers paid in dollars."[14]

On the 1978 mission, I was allowed to accompany my then husband, who was one of Geoffrey's economists. To Mariana, however, he confessed that he could not remember much about that mission "except for the fact that we were taken up to the northwest of the country for a weekend trip that was interesting."[15] It made a much deeper impression on me.

Corneliu's studio, which I, of course, visited, was extremely small. Nor was it heated or air-conditioned, as Corneliu complained to Geoffrey, who wrote back, "Still, you managed to exist there, to paint there and to gradually create a body of work that people have liked and of which you can be proud. It gave you access to some wonderful colleagues like [Ion] Musceleanu, the Gorduz, Pacea and others."[16] It was typical during the Ceaușescu years for artists to be assigned very small and very modest living quarters and studios. The Petrescus' apartment, which I also visited, appeared to be only one small room for them and an elderly parent.

Bucharest, conceived as the "Paris of the East," seemed to my American eye to be very run down. Geoffrey commented, "one could not look too closely at the dust on the streets and the disrepair of many of the buildings. Bucharest has many very nice private houses and mansions from the 19th century and pre-war 20th century. But the way they were treated after the war was a great pity. Chipped facades, wiring strung up the outside walls where the mansions had been converted into separate apartments."[17]

While the mission members were working during the day in meetings, tag-along spouses in most countries were left alone. This, however, was not the case in Communist Romania. A woman from the state's protocol office was assigned to look after me, accompanying me wherever I wanted to go. She was very interested in me, but our only common language was French, and if her questions became too personal I could fall back on "je ne comprends pas." Our hotel rooms were bugged, so that the *Securitate* (secret police) might record every burp; Fund business was discussed on sidewalks. In a Bucharest department store, it took me an inconceivably long time to find, arrange to pay for, actually pay for, and leave the store with an umbrella. I once got mistaken for a prostitute, perhaps because of my youthfulness and being on my own. I was sternly warned to avoid the black market. Queuing up for food looked like a lost cause, but I was able to buy small loaves of excellent peasant bread, crammed with seeds, nuts, and grains, for a pittance. On the weekend trip — which Geoffrey did recall — we were treated to enchantingly beautiful country, misty meanderings in deep forests and twisting mountain roads, and small peasant farms, spiriting us back to another time.

Romanian hospitality at mealtime was legendary: shots of țuică (a plum brandy of greatly varying quality) were insisted upon, often chased with beer. Traditional cuisine featured mămă-ligă (cornmeal porridge and sour cream), mititei (grilled sausage) and other meats, and sarmale (cabbage rolls), all washed down with quantities of Romanian wine, both red and white. It's hard to remember what I had for dessert. At official dinners, because of my knowledge of French, I would be seated next to the more elderly finance ministers who had been educated in the then language of diplomacy. These were fascinating evenings. Likewise, the evenings with the artists, often in their own ateliers, were less formal, charming and heartfelt, and we would leave them reluctantly at a very late hour.

Overall, as official guests, we were treated in a special way — eerily special, shielded from the dark realities of life under Ceaușescu's Communist rule — traveling in chauffeur-driven cars, bypassing queues, and undoubtedly much else that I didn't see. And it was from this place that Geoffrey brought away the artists' visions in their works, precious tokens of the Romanian spirit, now to be shown to the free world.

Decades passed. In 2008, thanks to a broken telephone line, Corneliu called me from Bucharest. He was frantically trying to contact Geoffrey, with whom he talked regularly but suddenly could not, and appealed to me. Thus I came back into Geoffrey's life. Our marriage seemed foreordained, and I owe my current joyous role as *chargée* of Geoffrey's grand purpose to Corneliu — and perhaps also to some squirrel who chewed the telephone wire. Together, Geoffrey and I decided upon and then arranged for his approximately eight-hundred-work art collection to go to his alma mater, the University of Tasmania. Even in his large house, the treasures had piled up over the years. Artworks were hung on the walls in vertical stacks, and when that space was used up, they were back-to-back and front-to-front against walls and furniture, or stored in portfolios under beds and in drawers and closets. Many times I drew upon the resources of my former colleagues at the Smithsonian's National Portrait Gallery for advice about how to convey the collection there safely and properly accounted for, and the myriad other professional tasks of museums. Geoffrey continued to report on all of this to Corneliu's widow Mariana, who shared in his triumph. Both have left us now.

It is truly extraordinary to me that so much beauty has sprung from such dark times in Romania, and that is what this book wishes to capture. Art speaks its own language. It stands apart from other records of those times, abundantly addressed from the standpoints of history, politics, social sciences, and literature. The art presented in this book represents a very small fraction of Geoffrey's collection: these are the works I have kept for myself, for now, to grace my house here in

Washington, DC, and to share with all who visit me. The core collection resides in the care of the University of Tasmania in Hobart. There, one can see not only many more works by the artists in this book but also by more Romanian artists. Traveling to Hobart is a long hop for many of us, though. From Washington I must cross fourteen or fifteen time zones, and this will take several days, depending upon stopovers and one's comfort level. During the current pandemic, even this is not possible. The internet has come to the rescue and, indeed, thanks to the outstanding creation of the Tyler Collection Research Repository by Curator Rachael Rose at the University of Tasmania, there is much to find. The search can begin here.

Catalogue Plates

Geoffrey collected hundreds of artworks by Corneliu Petrescu. These make up the bulk of his collection, as in turn they do mine. Selected works are shown here.

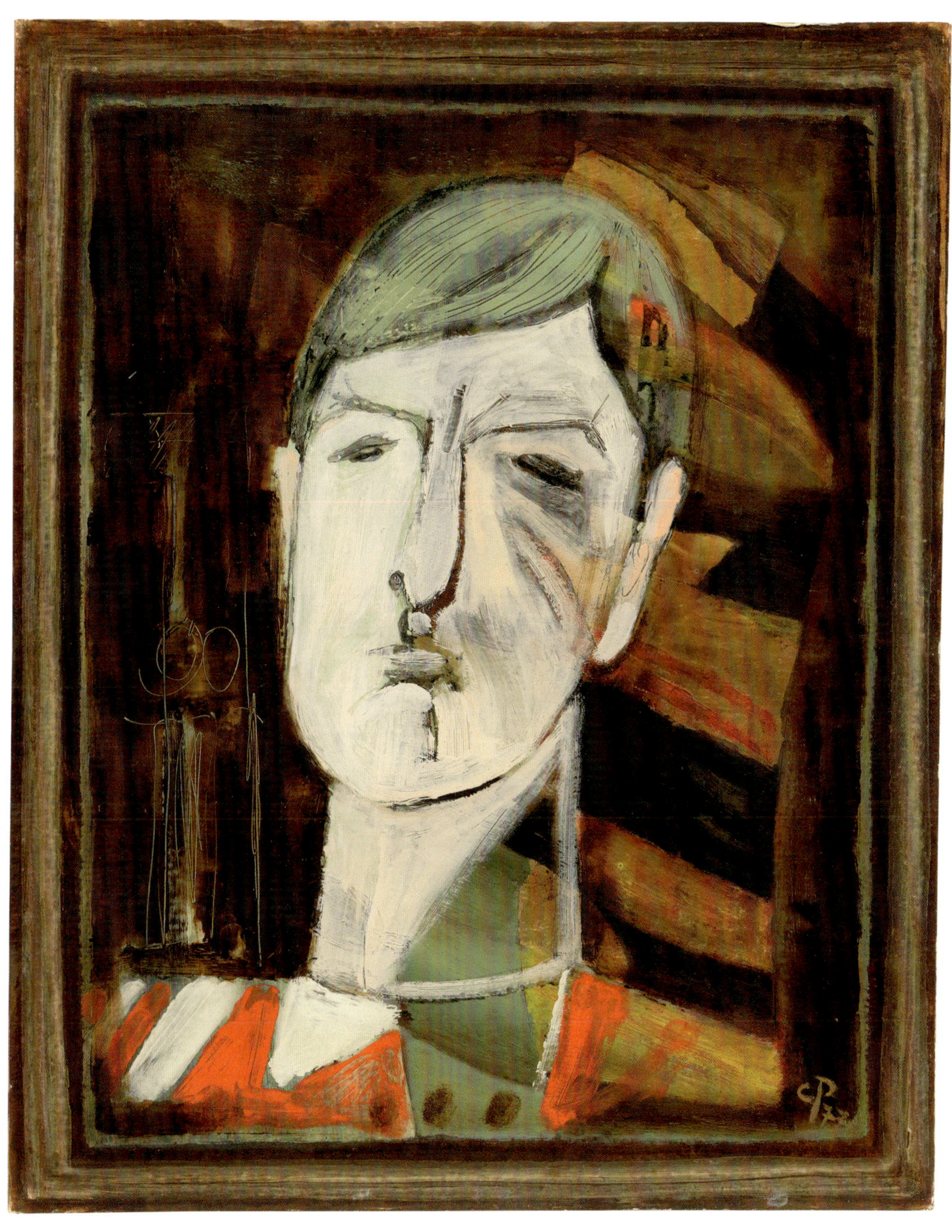

Corneliu Petrescu, *Portrait of Geoffrey Tyler* (cat. 34)

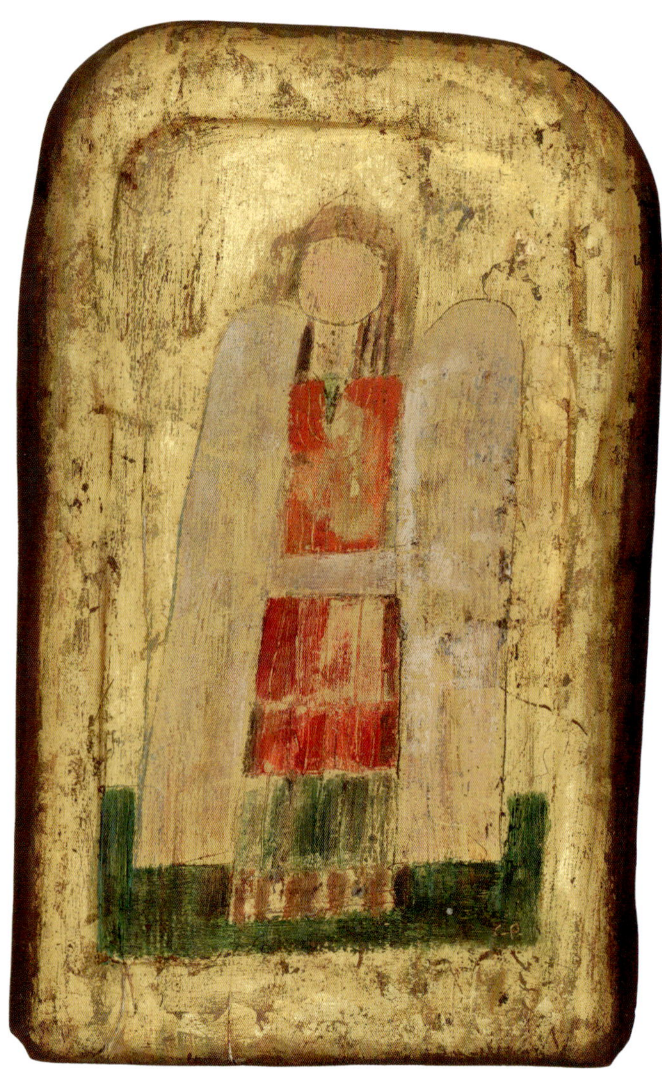

Corneliu Petrescu, *Angel* (cat. 21)

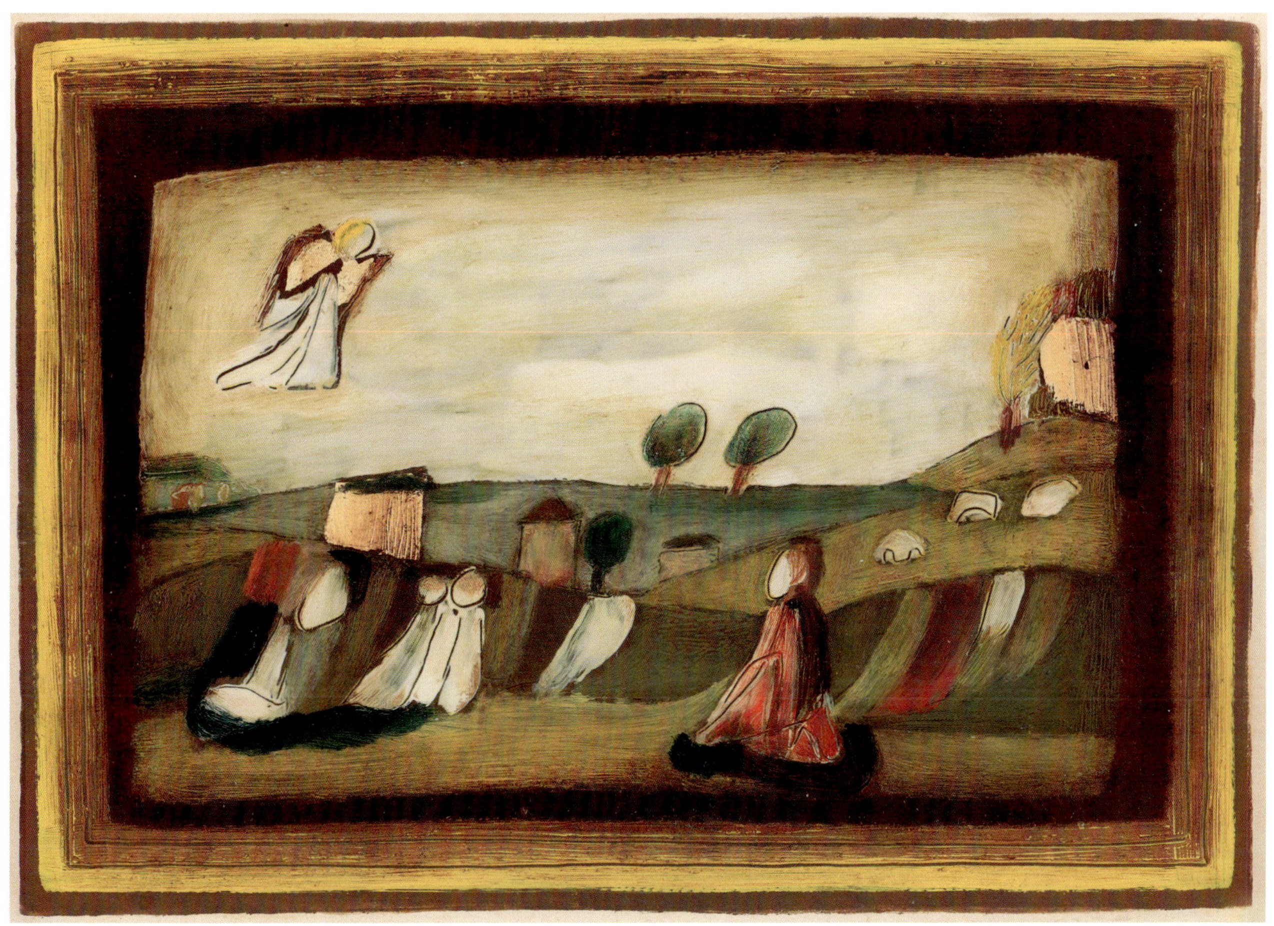

Corneliu Petrescu, *Angel in Sky* (cat. 18)

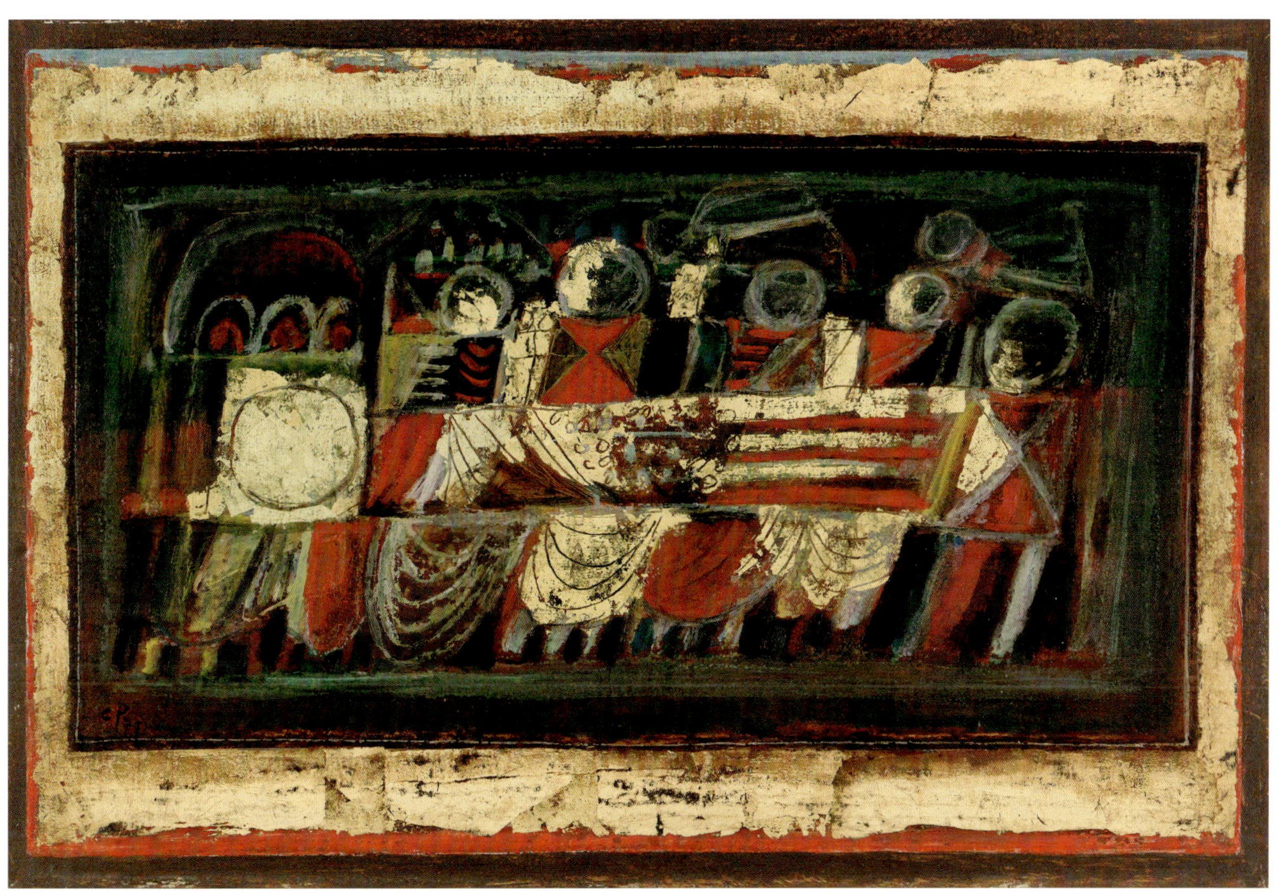

Corneliu Petrescu, *Untitled* (cat. 35)

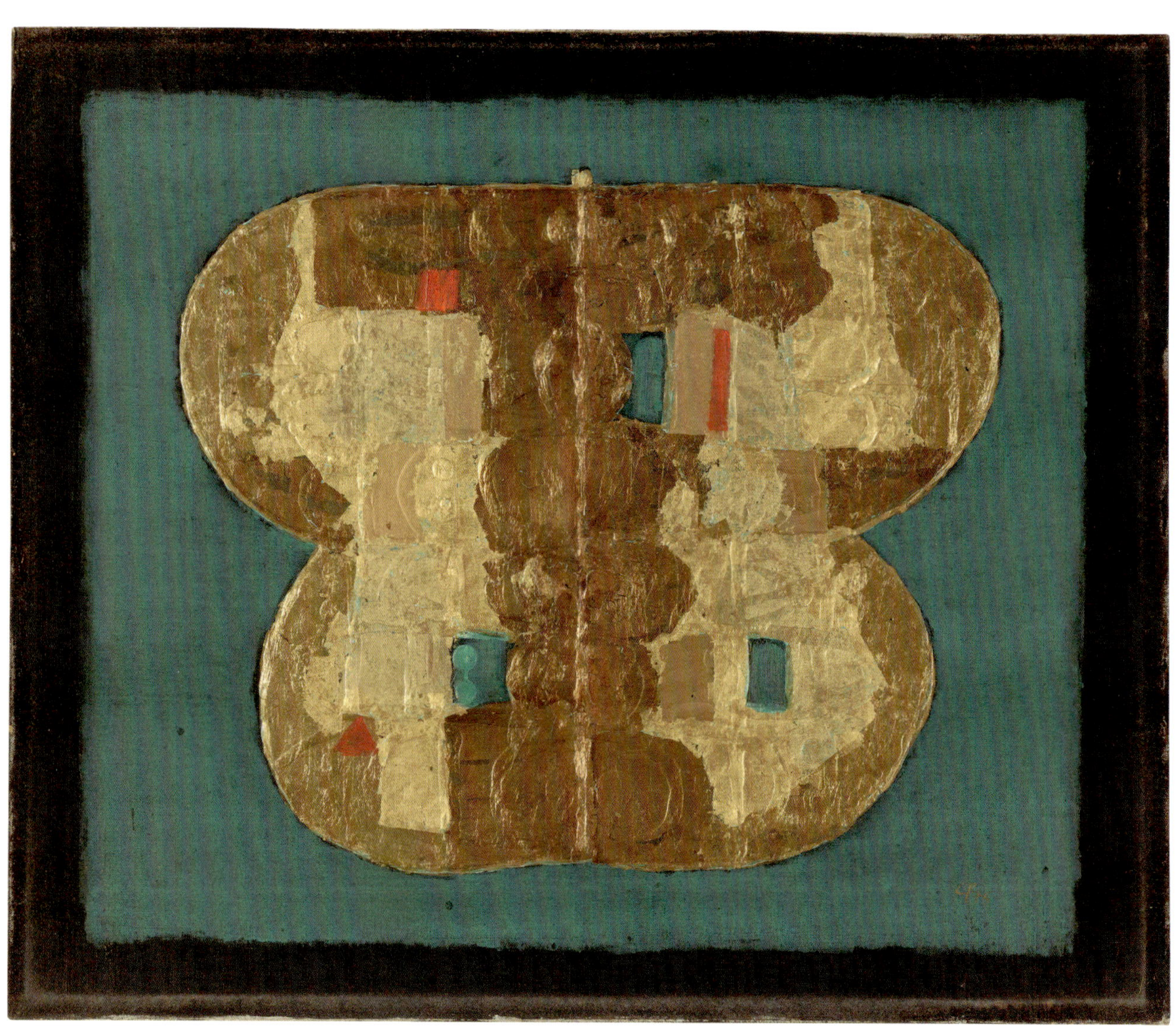

Corneliu Petrescu, *Fluture (Butterfly)* (cat. 26)

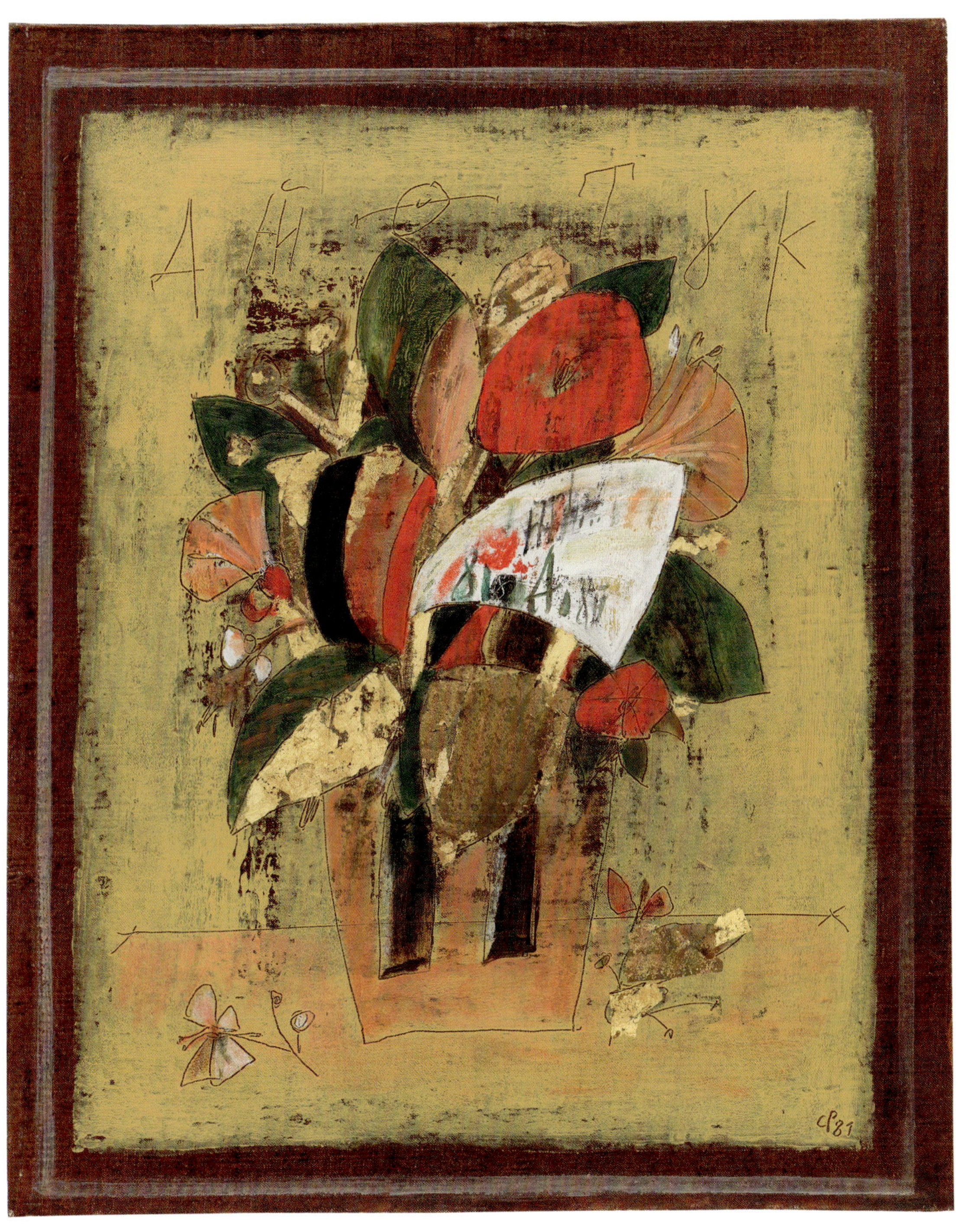

Corneliu Petrescu, *Flowers* (cat. 47)

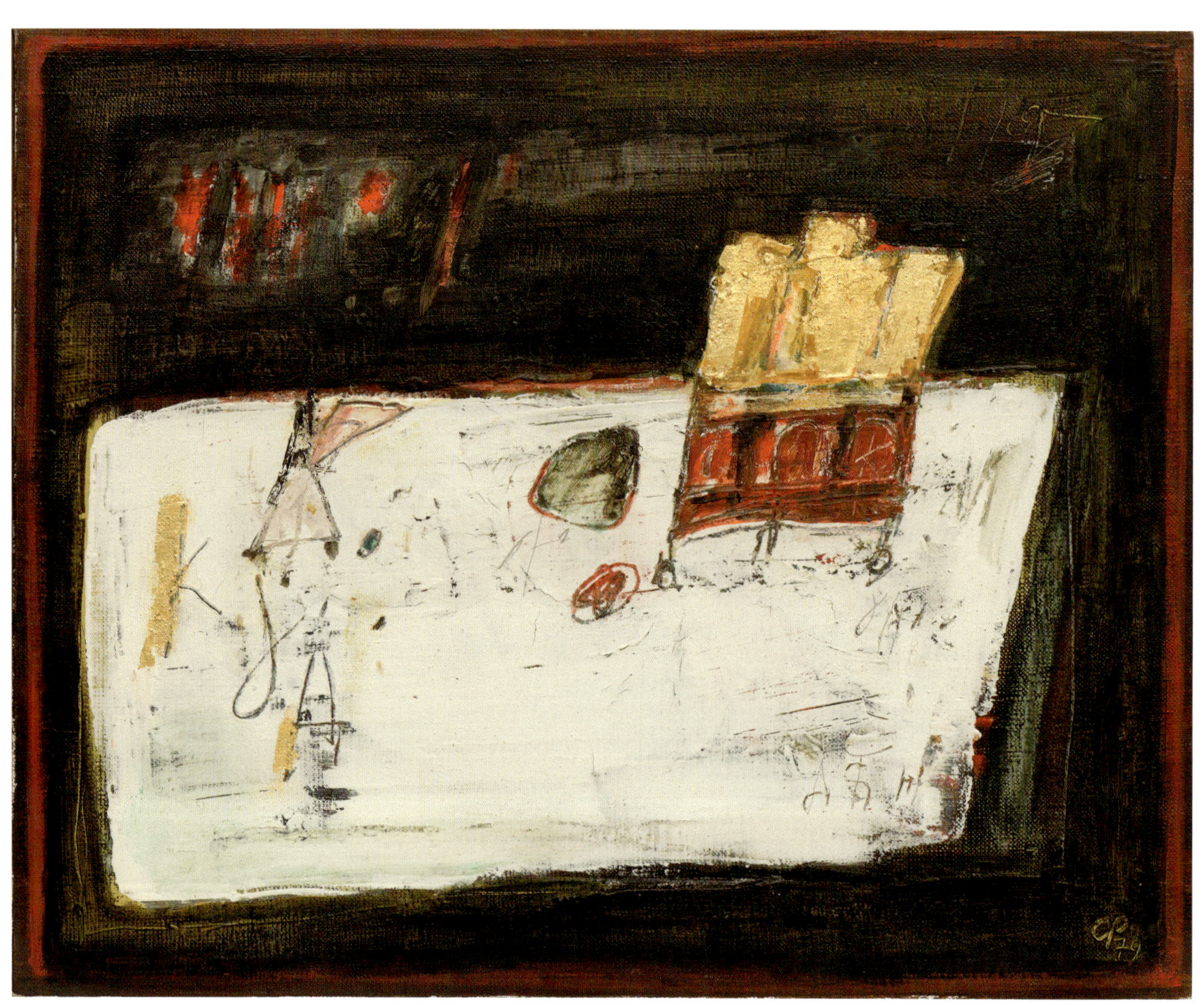

Corneliu Petrescu, *Untitled* (cat. 42)

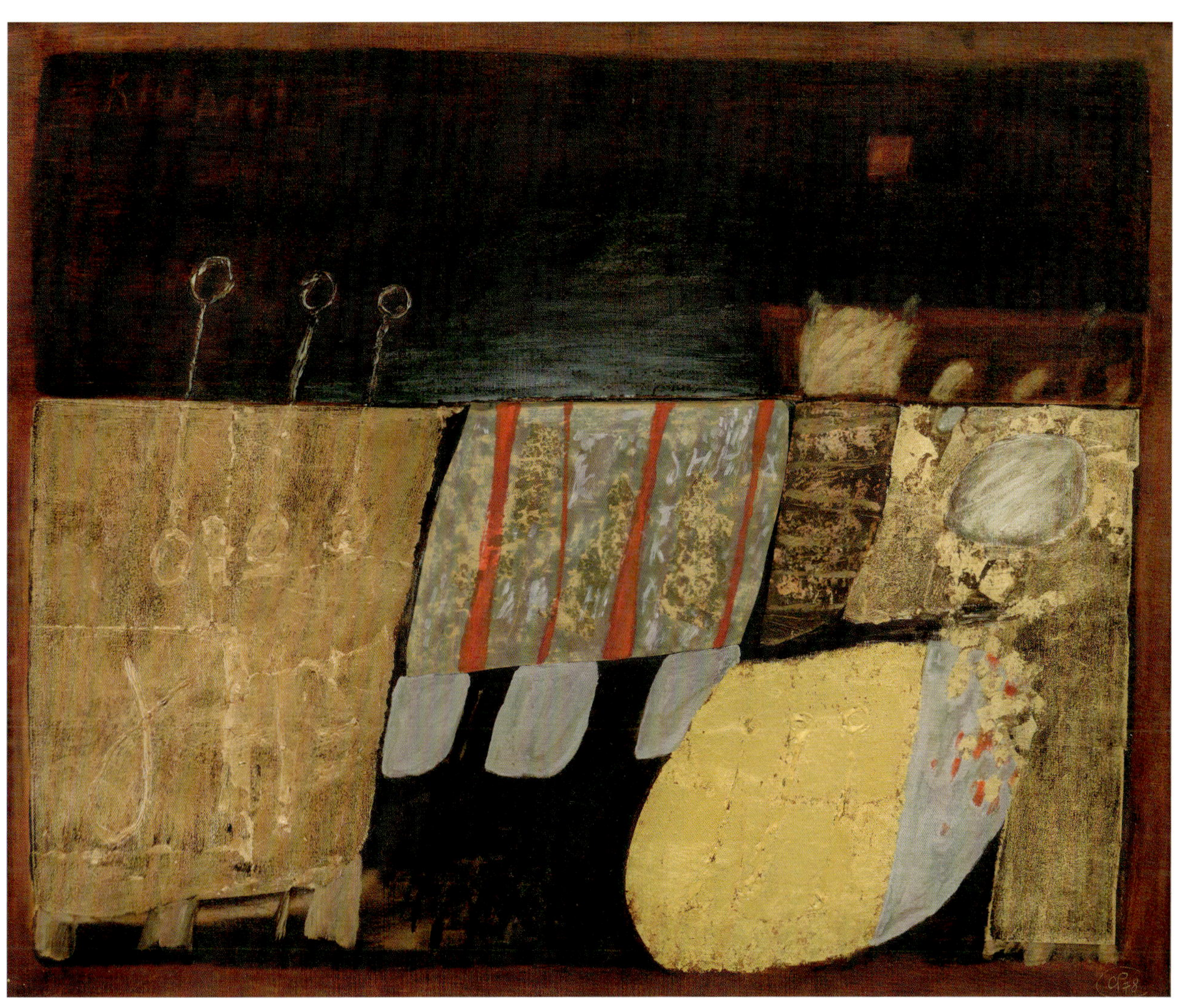

Corneliu Petrescu, *Untitled* (cat. 39)

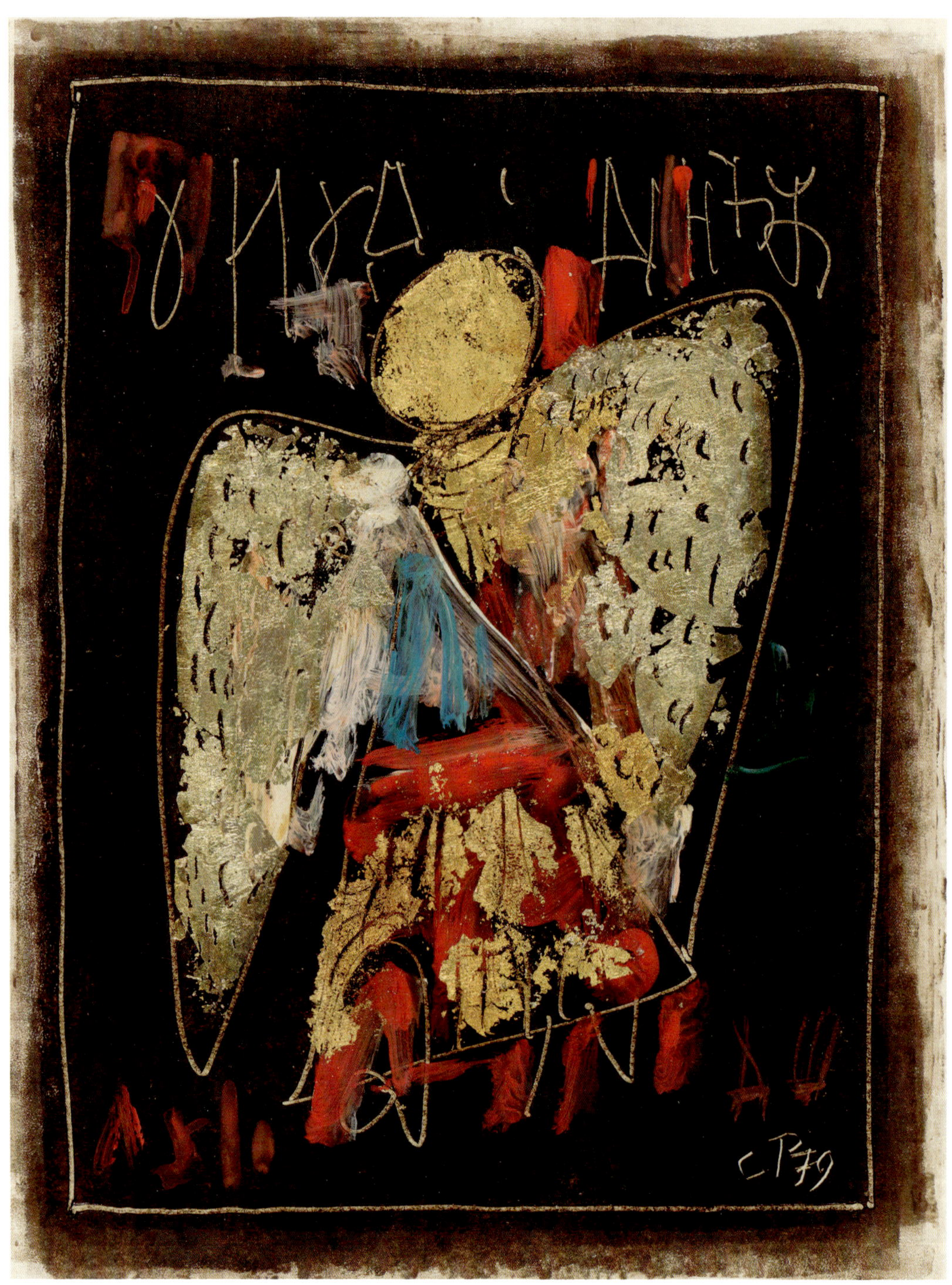

Corneliu Petrescu, *Angel* (cat. 40)

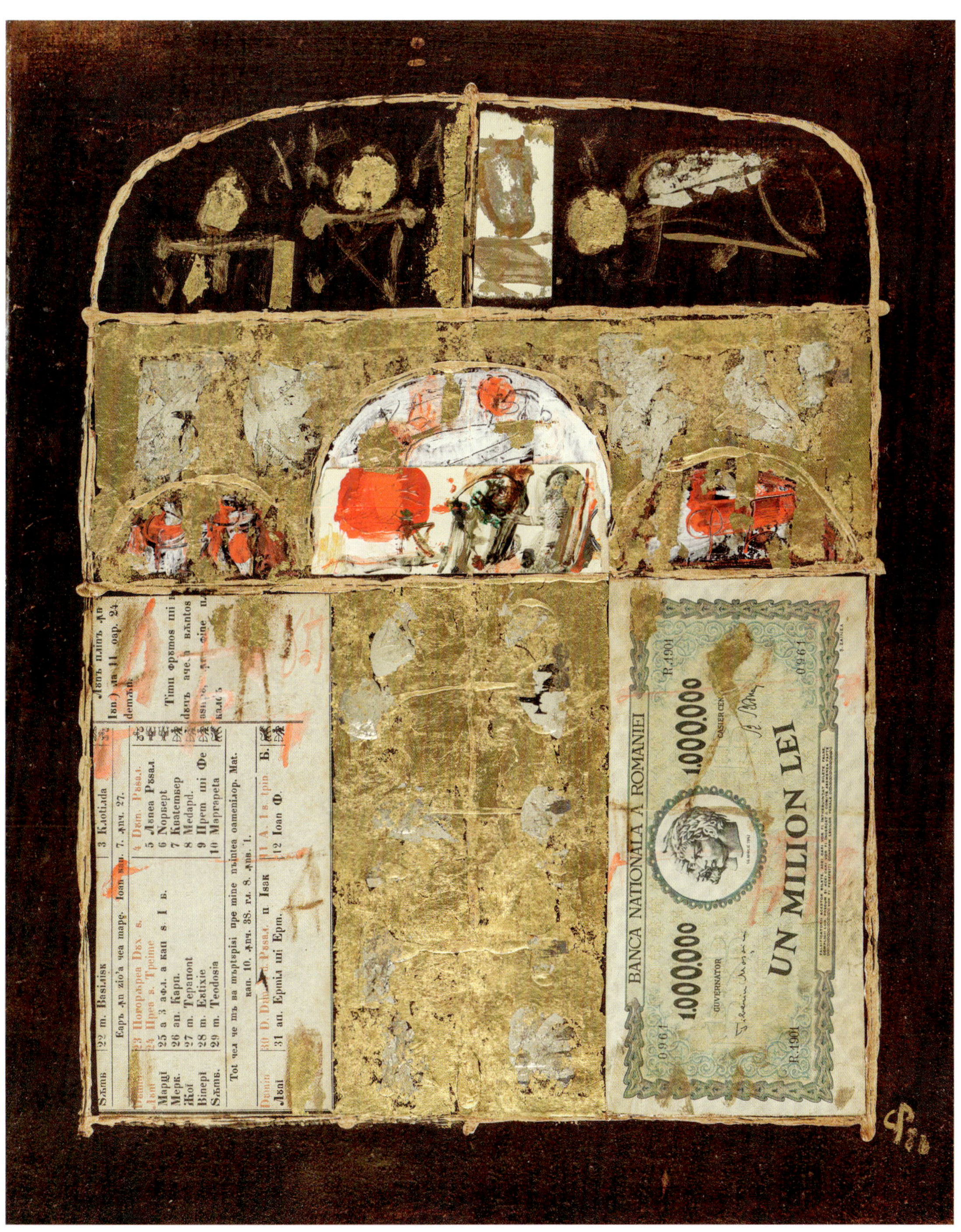

Corneliu Petrescu, *Icon* (cat. 45)

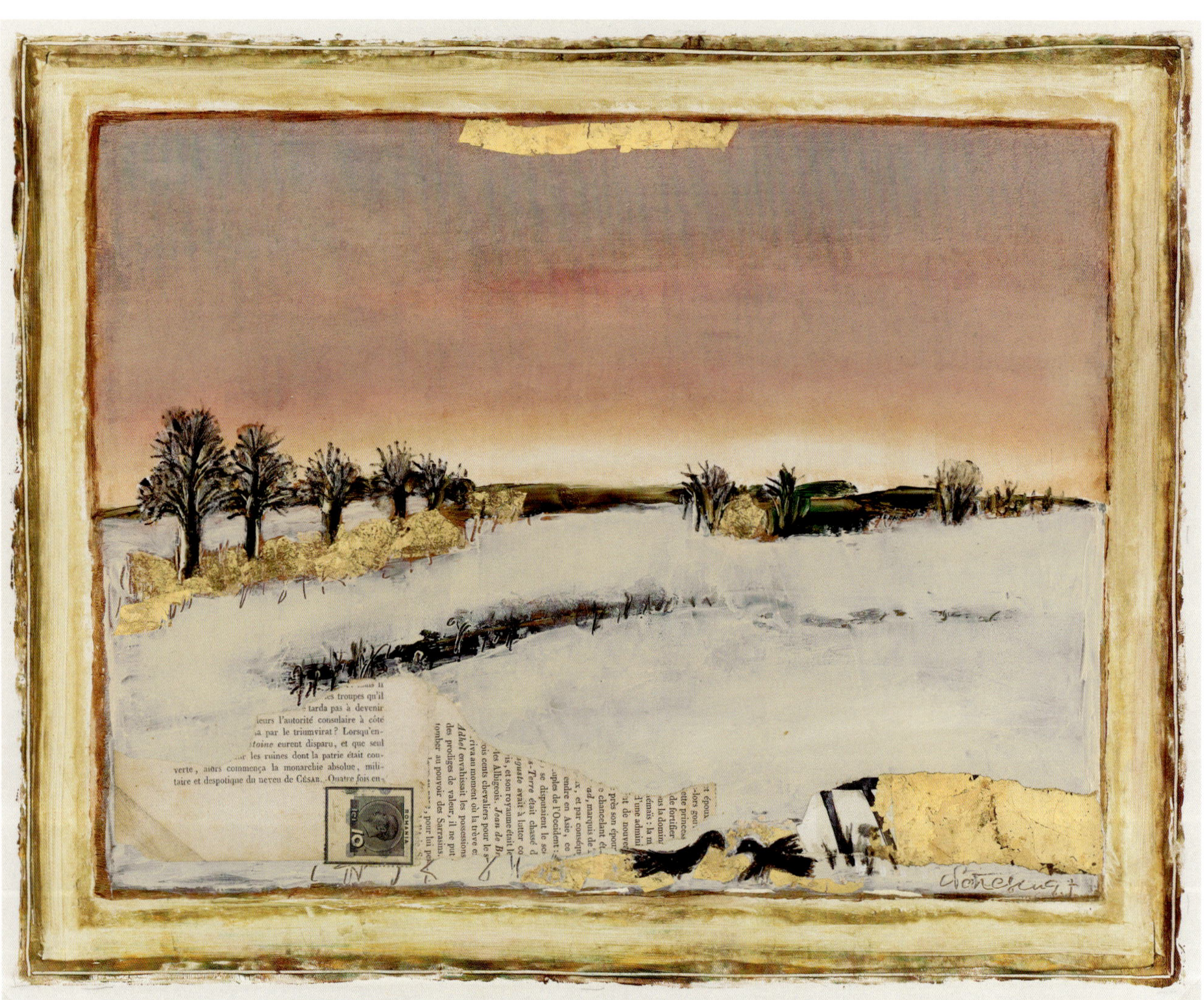

Corneliu Petrescu, *Winter* (cat. 57)

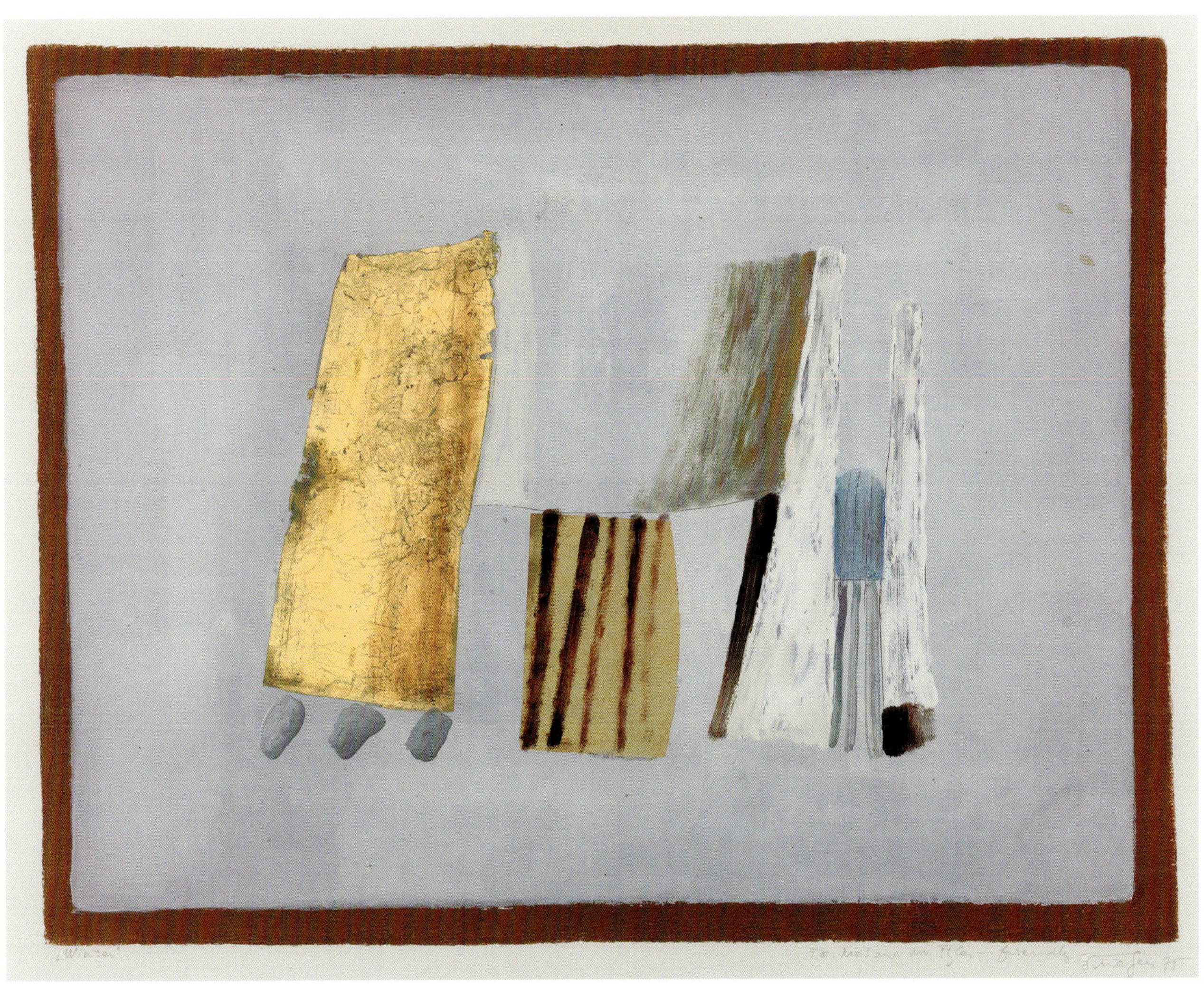

Corneliu Petrescu, *Winter* (cat. 28)

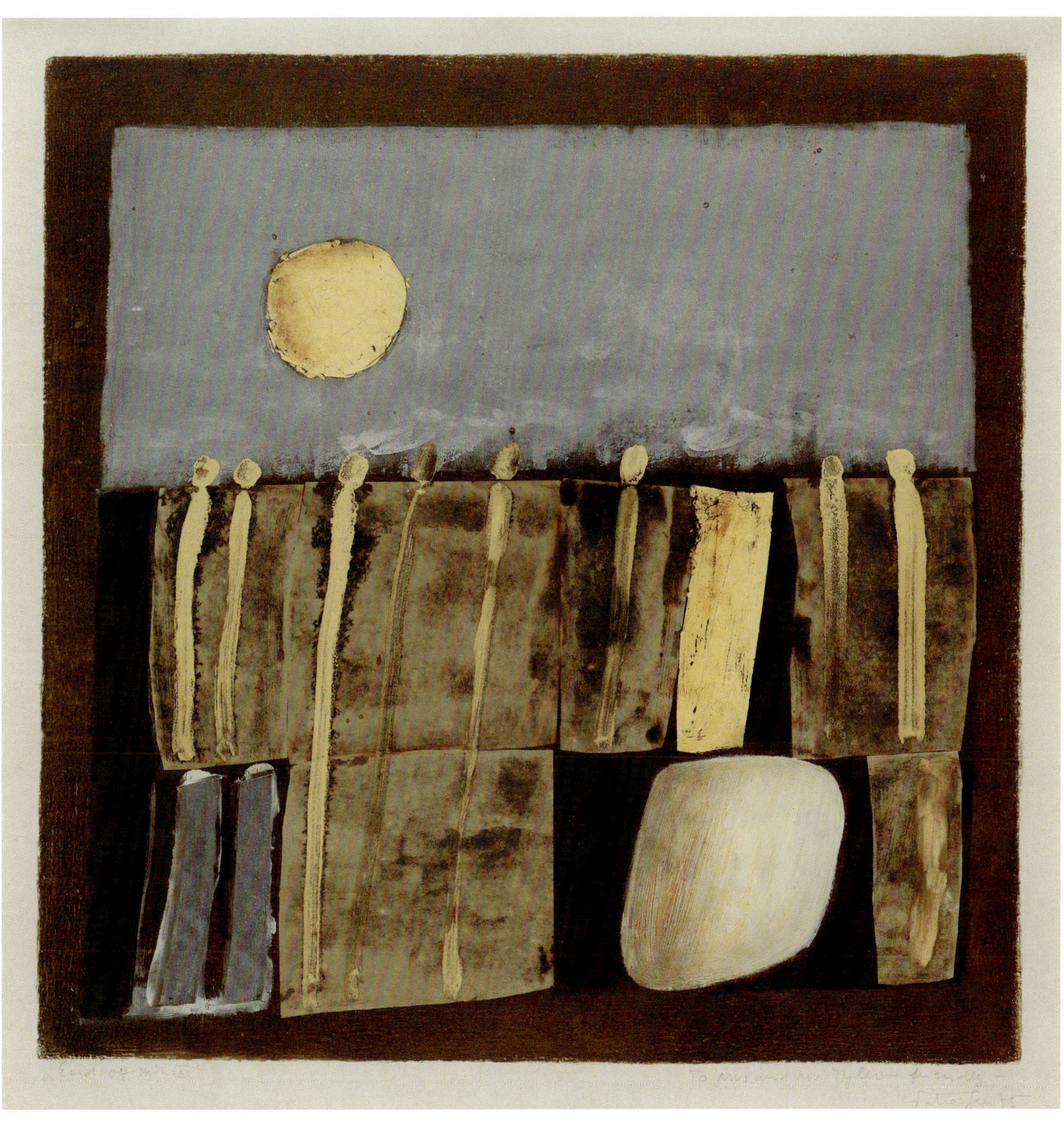

Corneliu Petrescu, *End of Winter* (cat. 29)

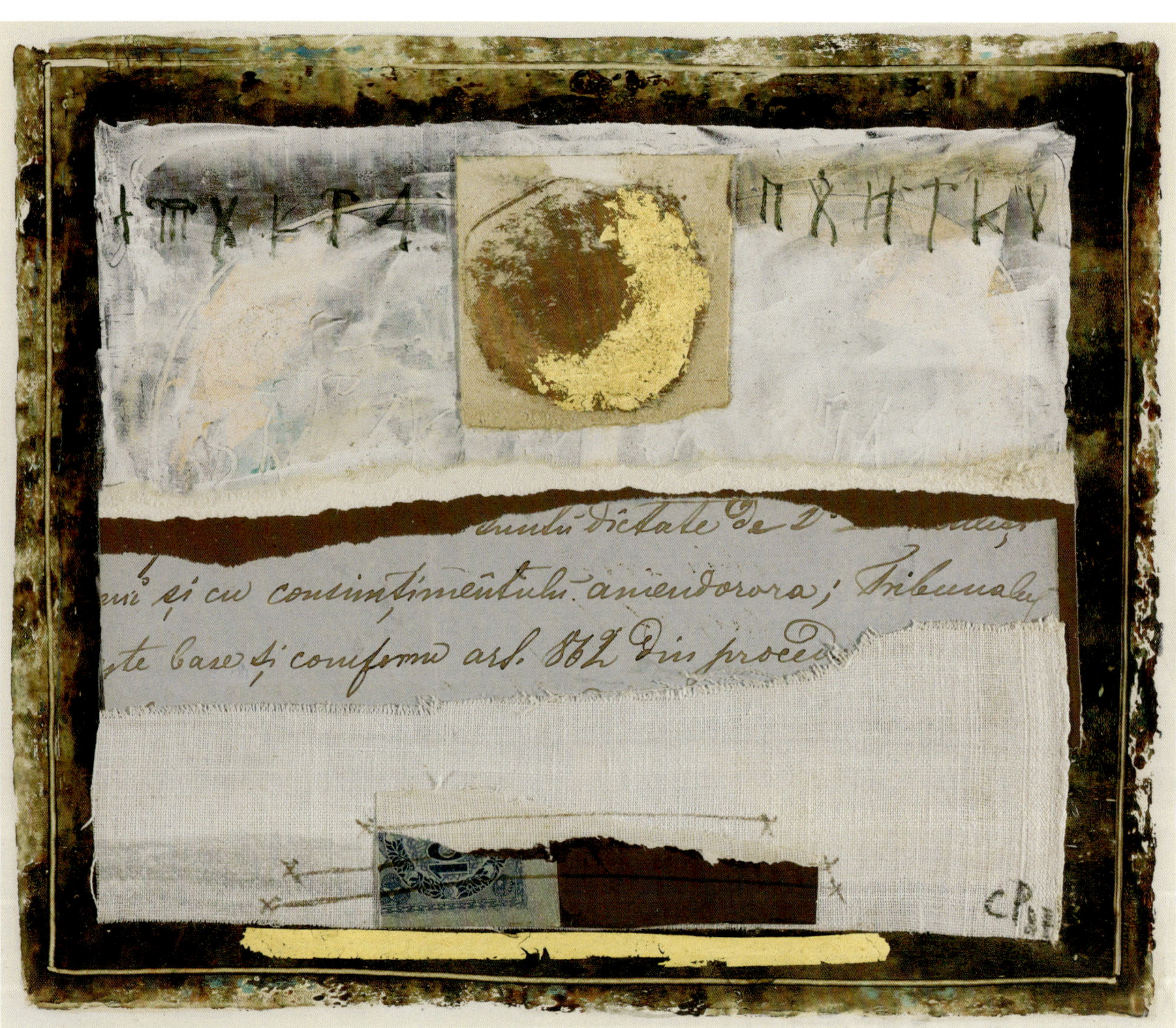

Corneliu Petrescu, *Landscape* (cat. 50)

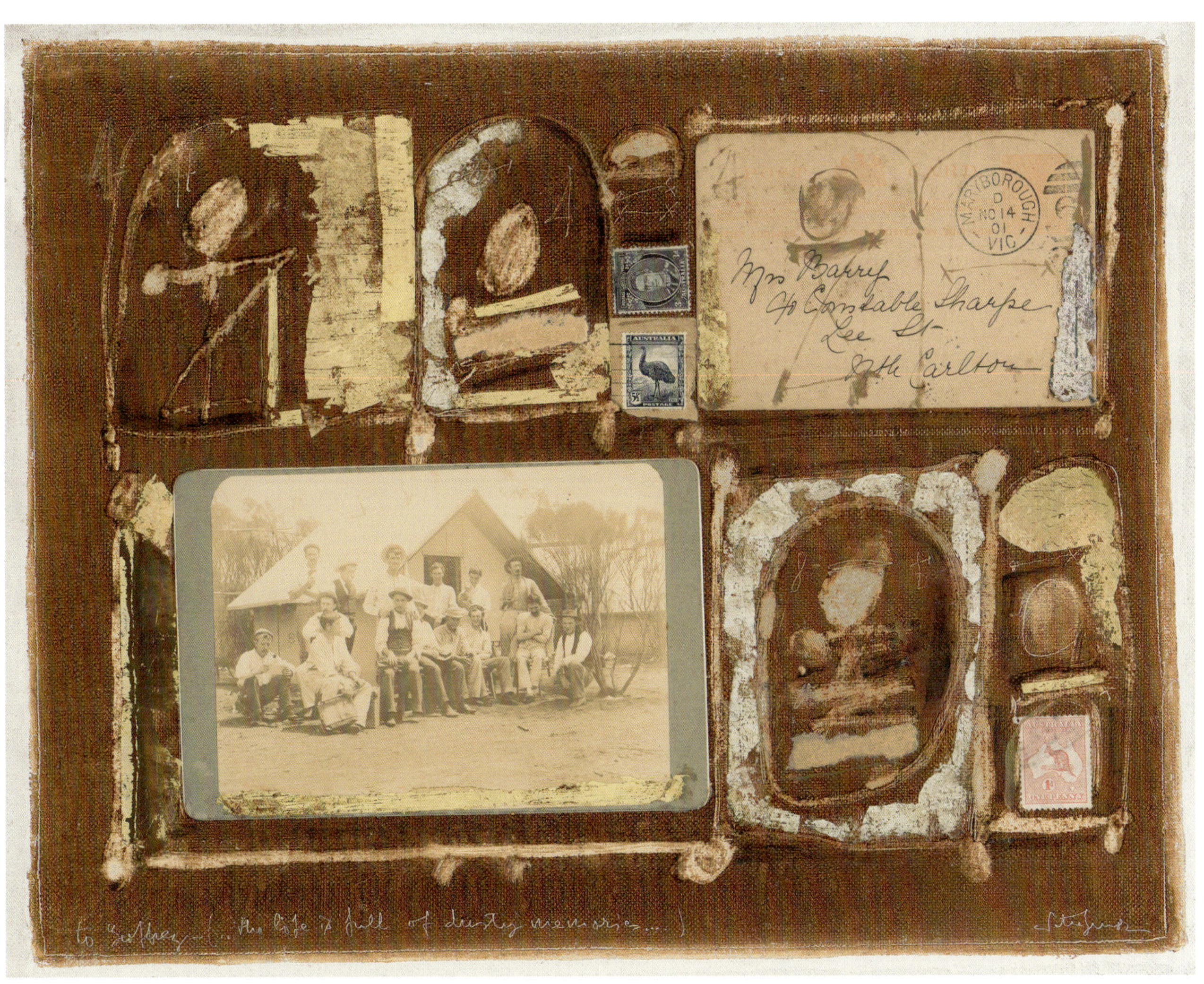

Corneliu Petrescu, *Dusty Memories* (cat. 48)

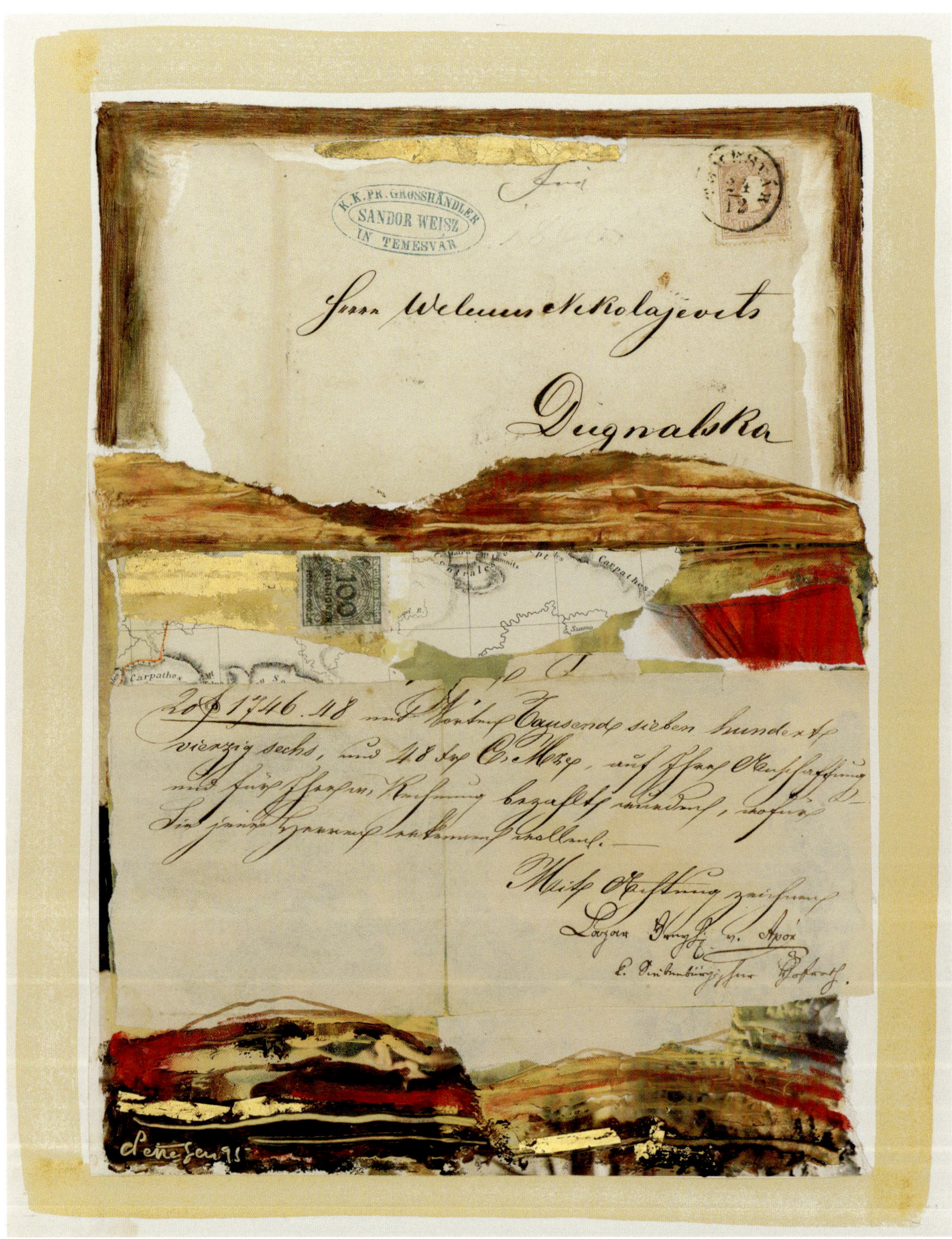

Corneliu Petrescu, *Desert* (cat. 53)

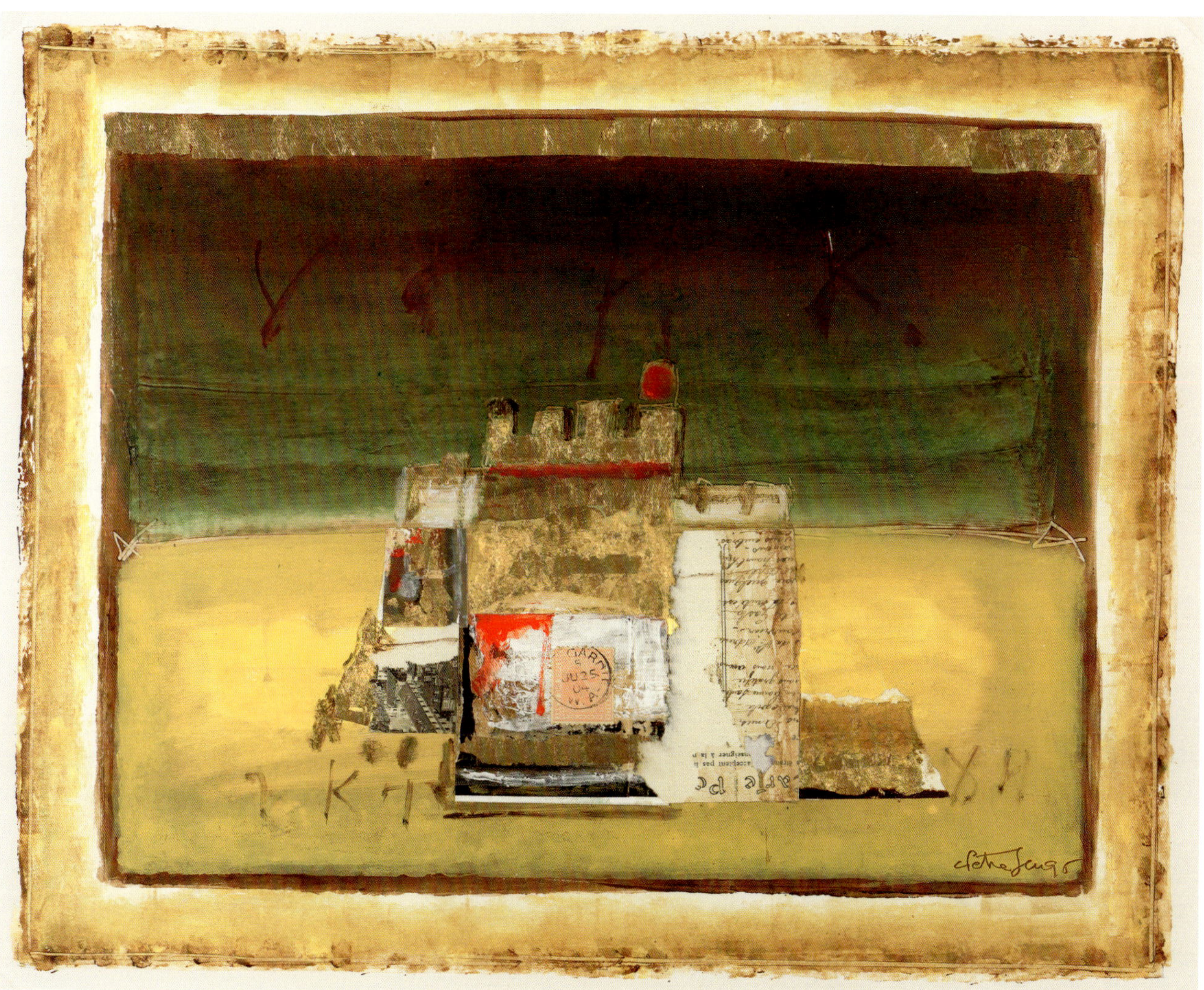

Corneliu Petrescu, *Sandcastle* (cat. 51)

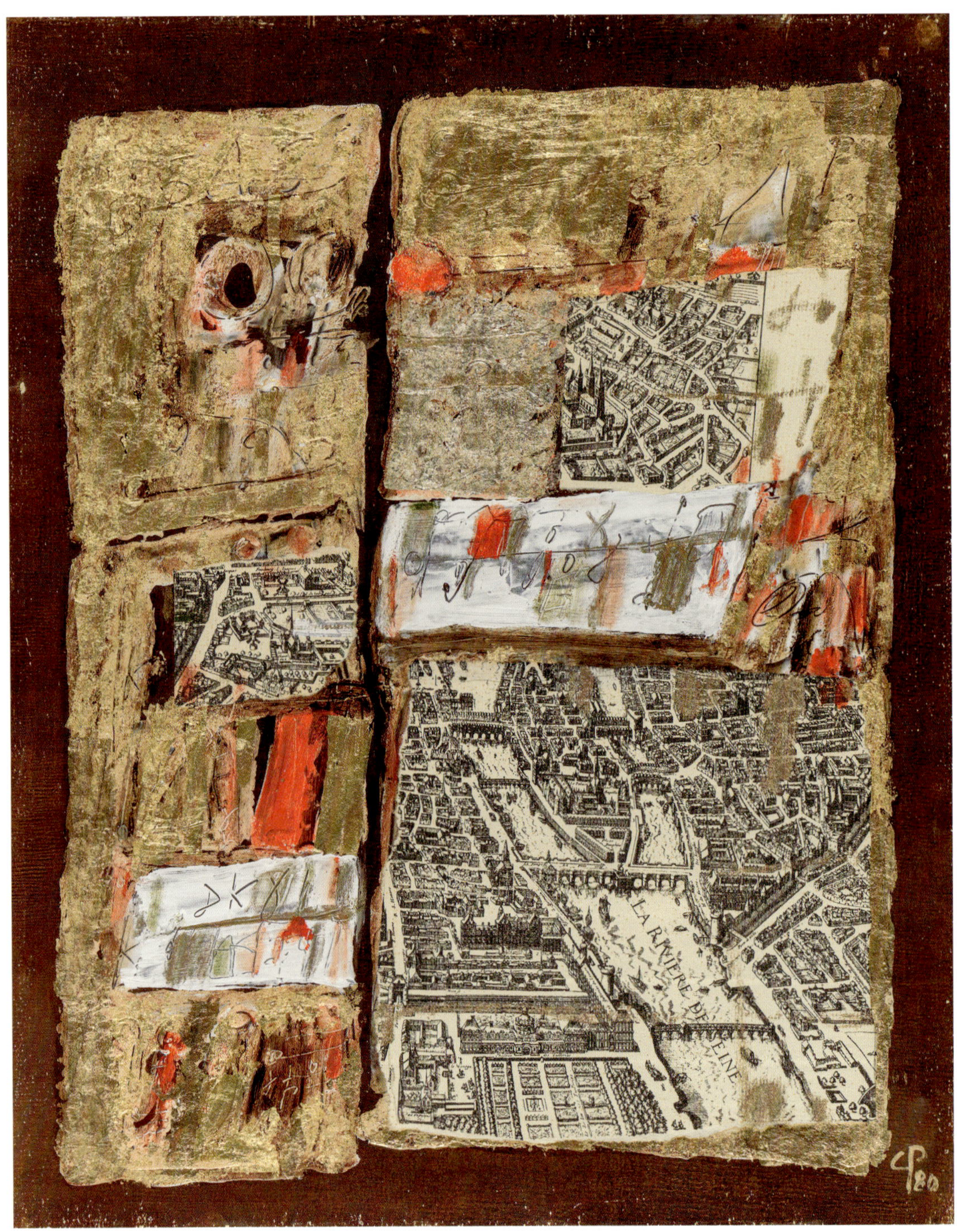

Corneliu Petrescu, *Untitled* (cat. 46)

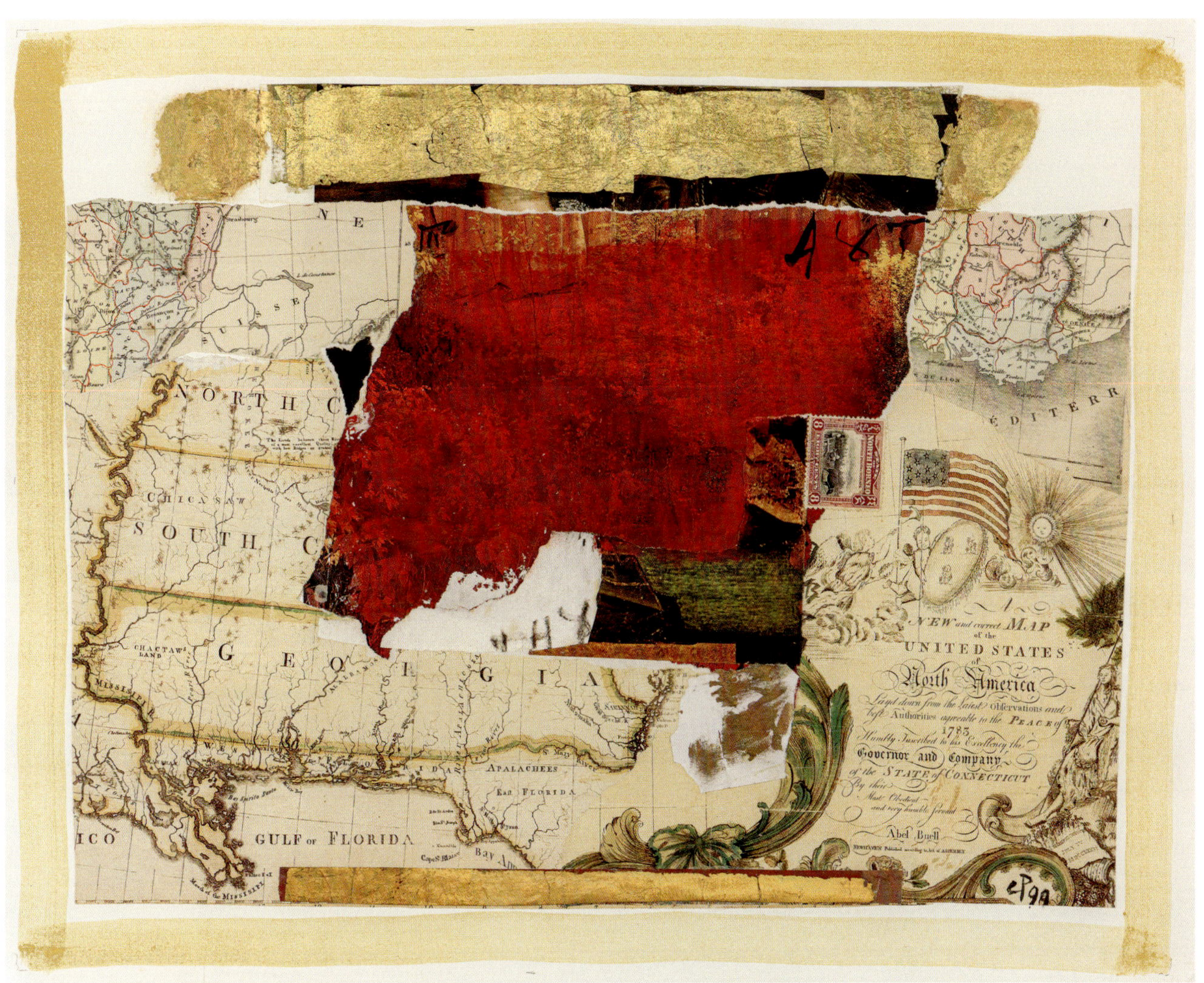

Corneliu Petrescu, *Untitled* (cat. 60)

Petrescu was not regarded as an artist of the first
rank himself, lacking formal education and
launching his career late in life. To make Geoffrey's
collection as representative of the Ceauşescu
period as possible, he turned to others, notably the
sculptor Gorduz and his wife, ceramist Silvia Radu.
Both were prominent and well connected in the
art world. As a result, Geoffrey's collection includes
works by many of the most distinguished artists
of that time.

Horia Bernea
Ştefan Câlţia
Marin Gherasim
Vasile Gorduz
Marcel Guguianu
Sorin Ilfoveanu
Georgeta Năpăruş
Ion Nicodim
Ion Pacea
Silvia Radu
Gheorghe Şaru
Icon workshop

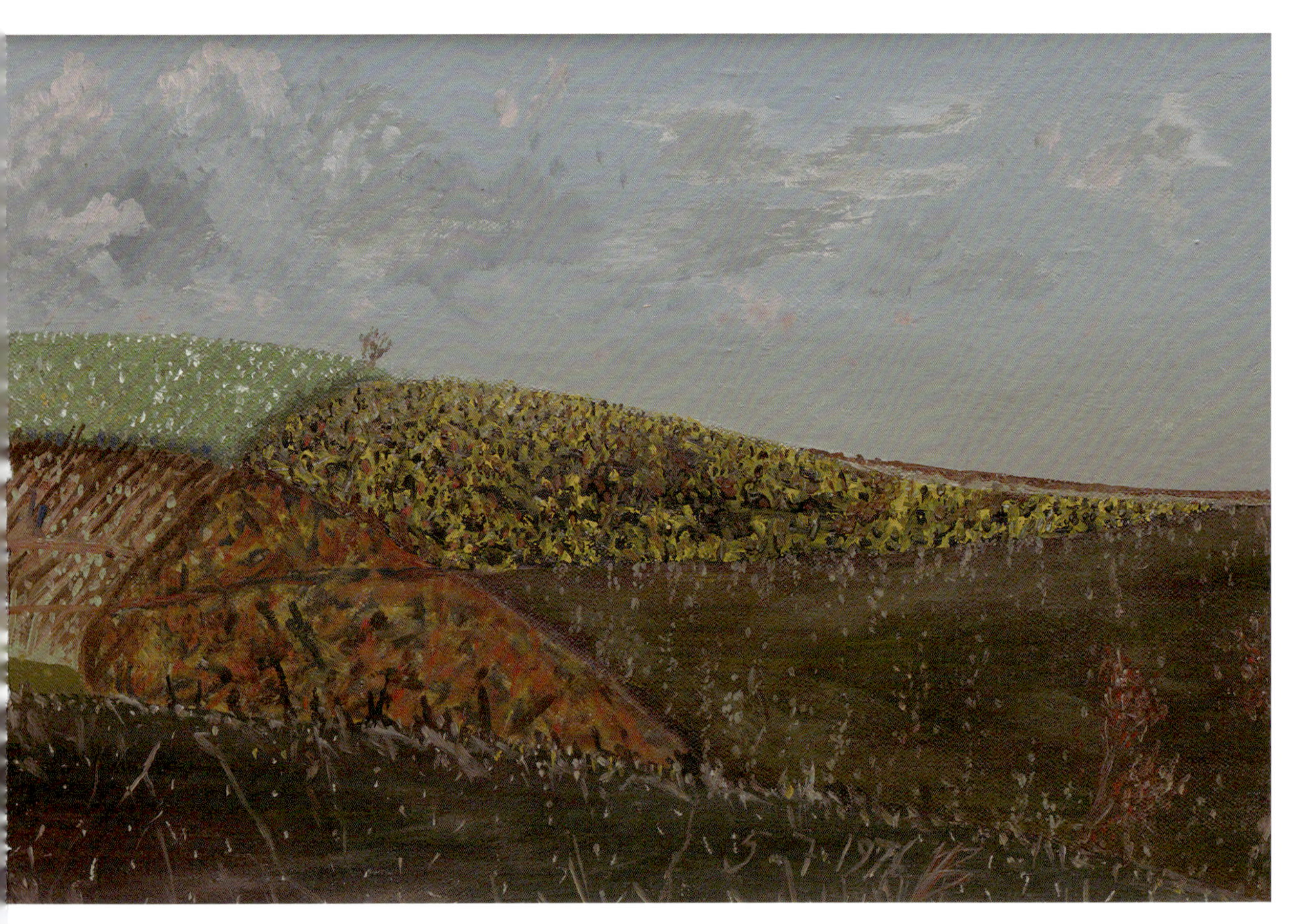

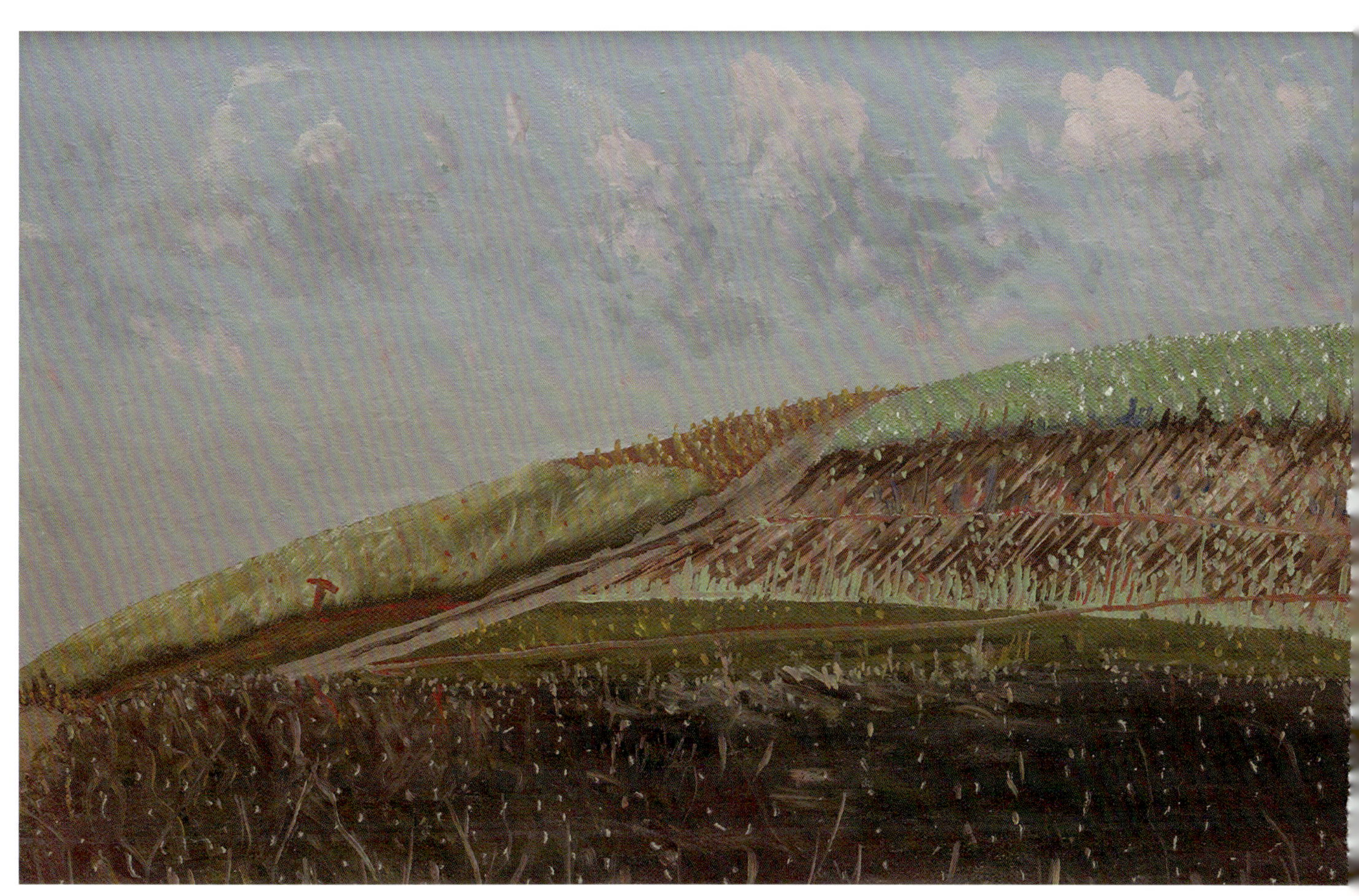

Horia Bernea, *Study for "Hill V"* (cat. 1)

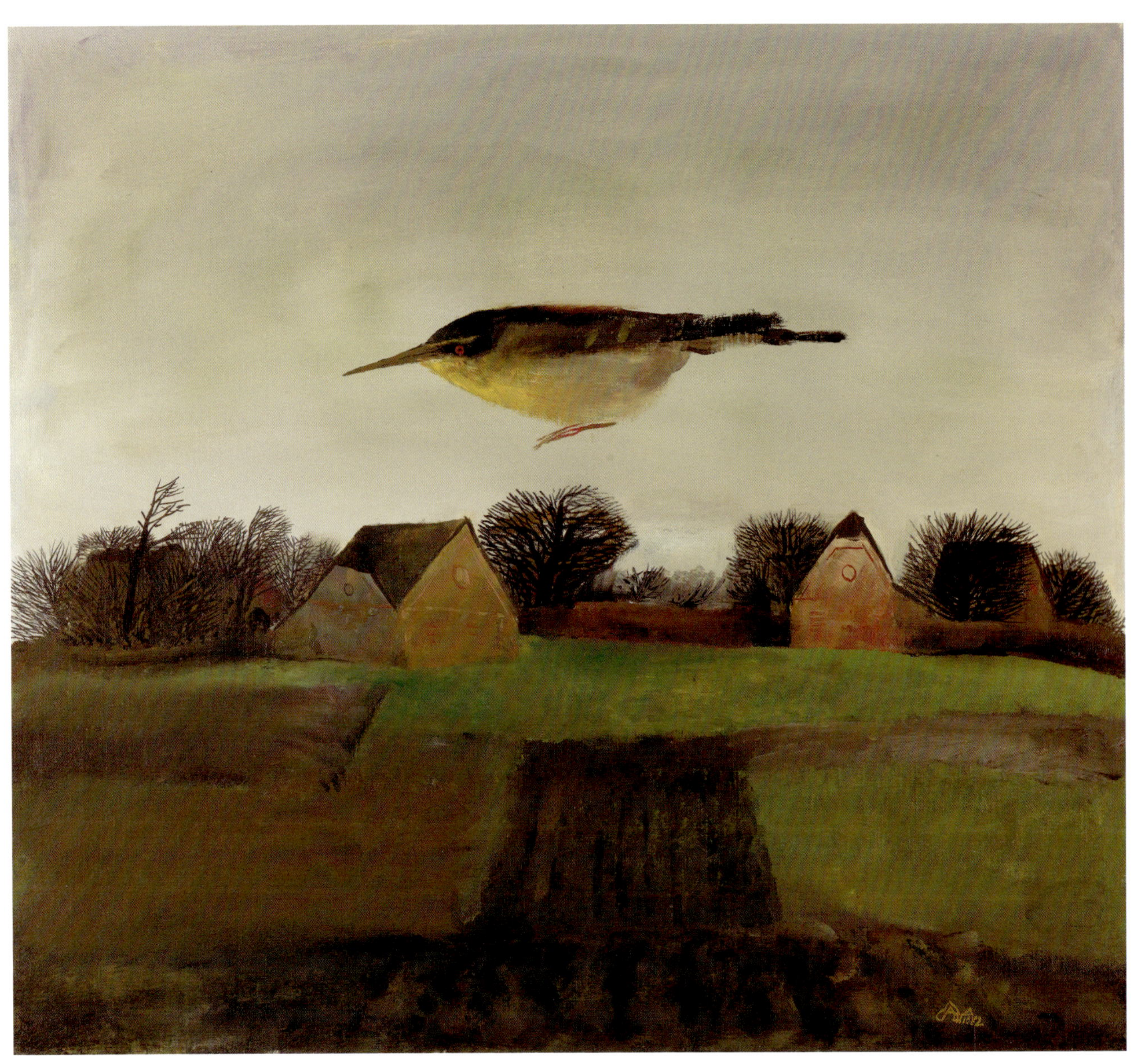

Ştefan Câlţia, *Cottage and Bird* (cat. 4)

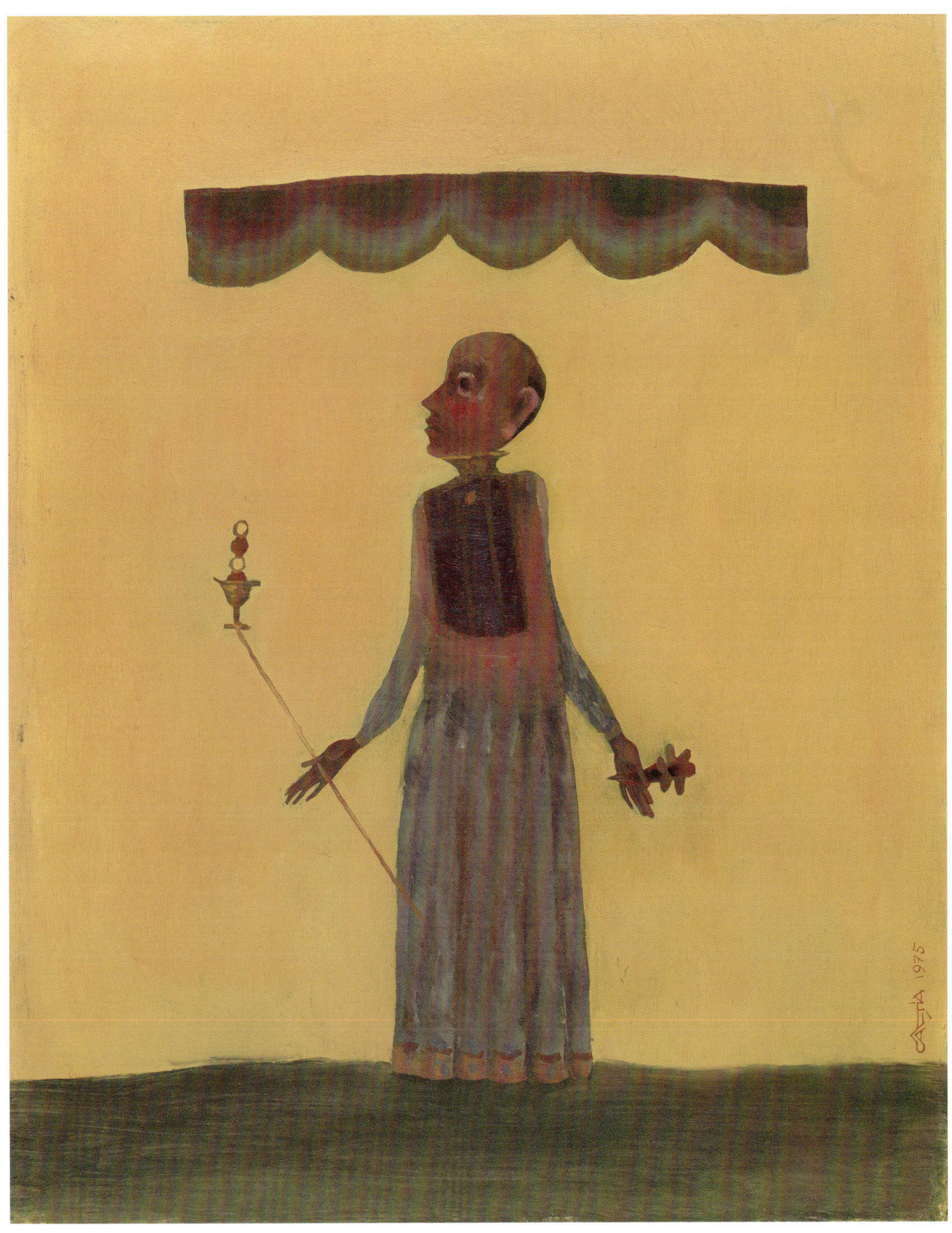

Ştefan Câlţia, *Bărbat in Spectacol (Man in a Show)* (cat. 2)

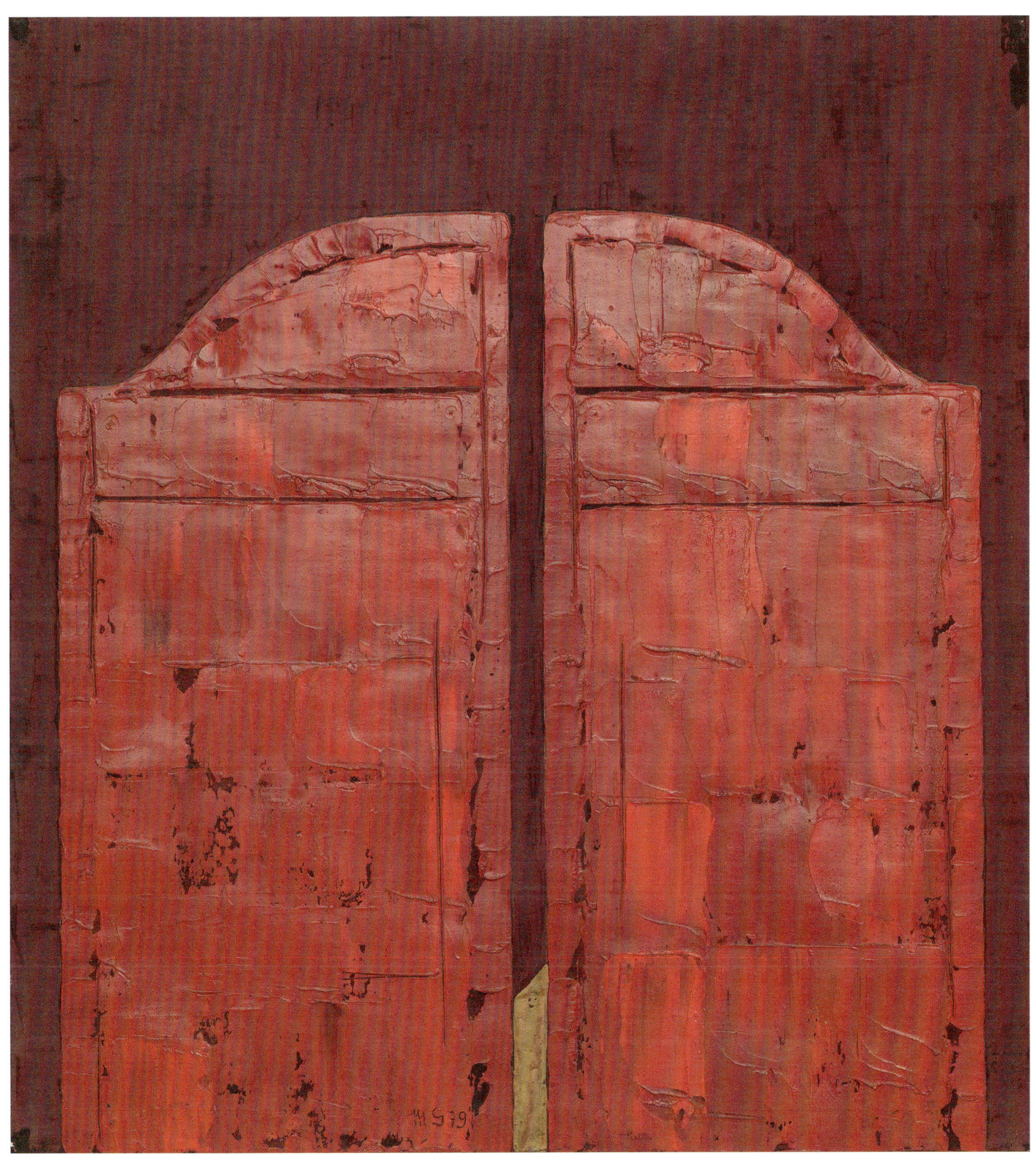

Marin Gherasim, *Poărta Jertfelor (Gate of the Sacrifices)* (cat. 5)

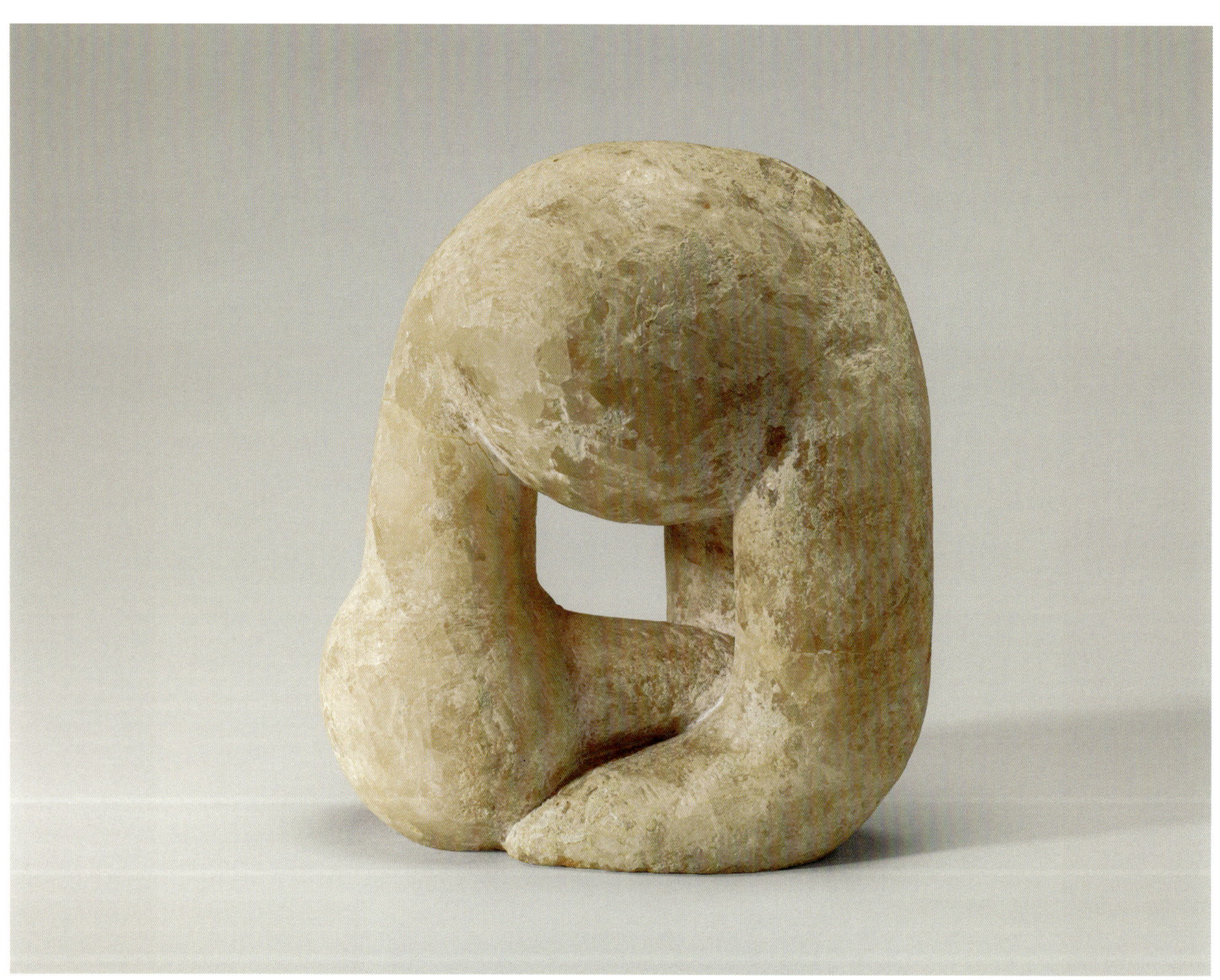

Vasile Gorduz, *Ordinary Bird (Bird Sleeping)* (cat. 6)

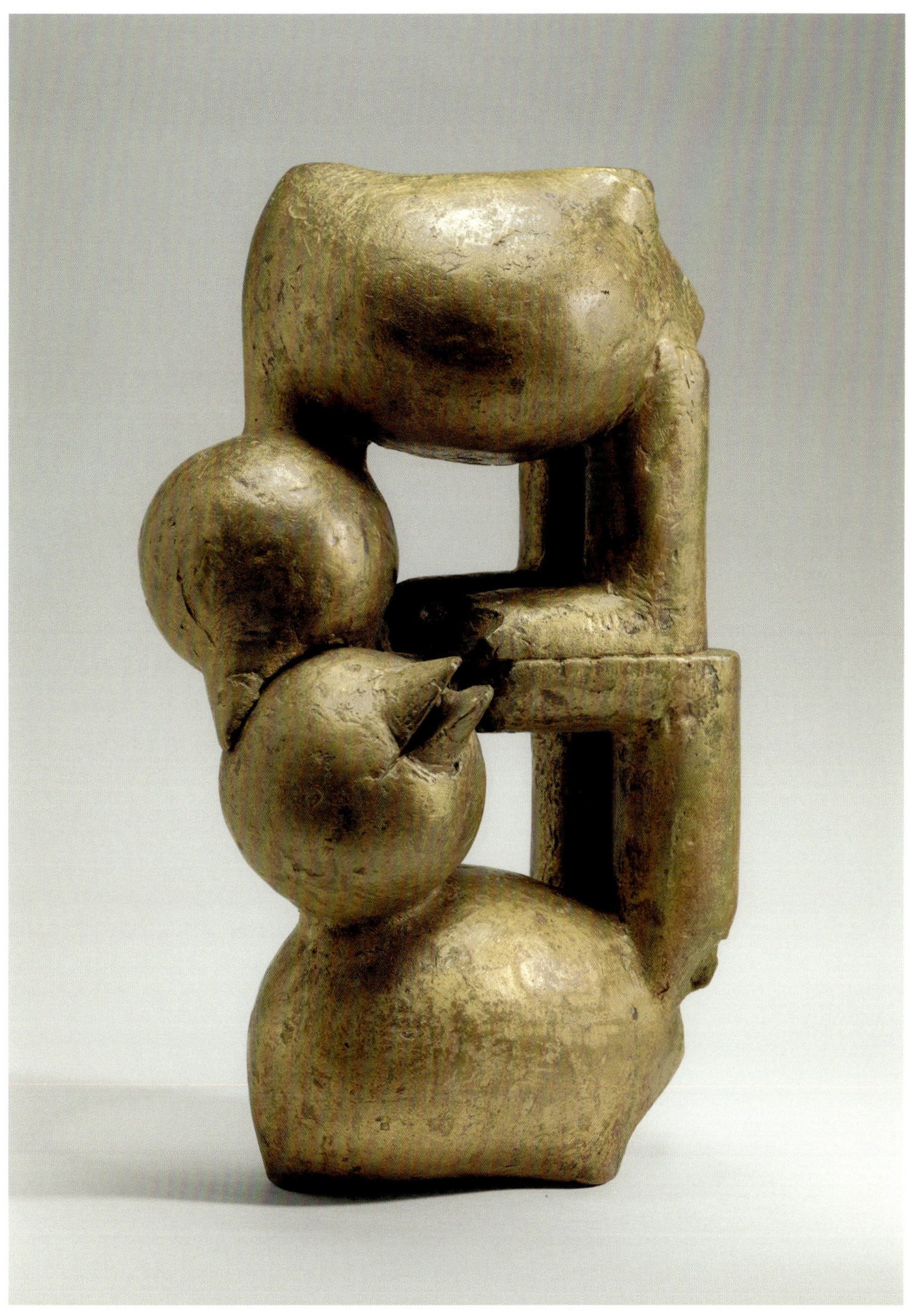

Vasile Gorduz, *Bird Swallowing Its Own Shadow* (cat. 8)

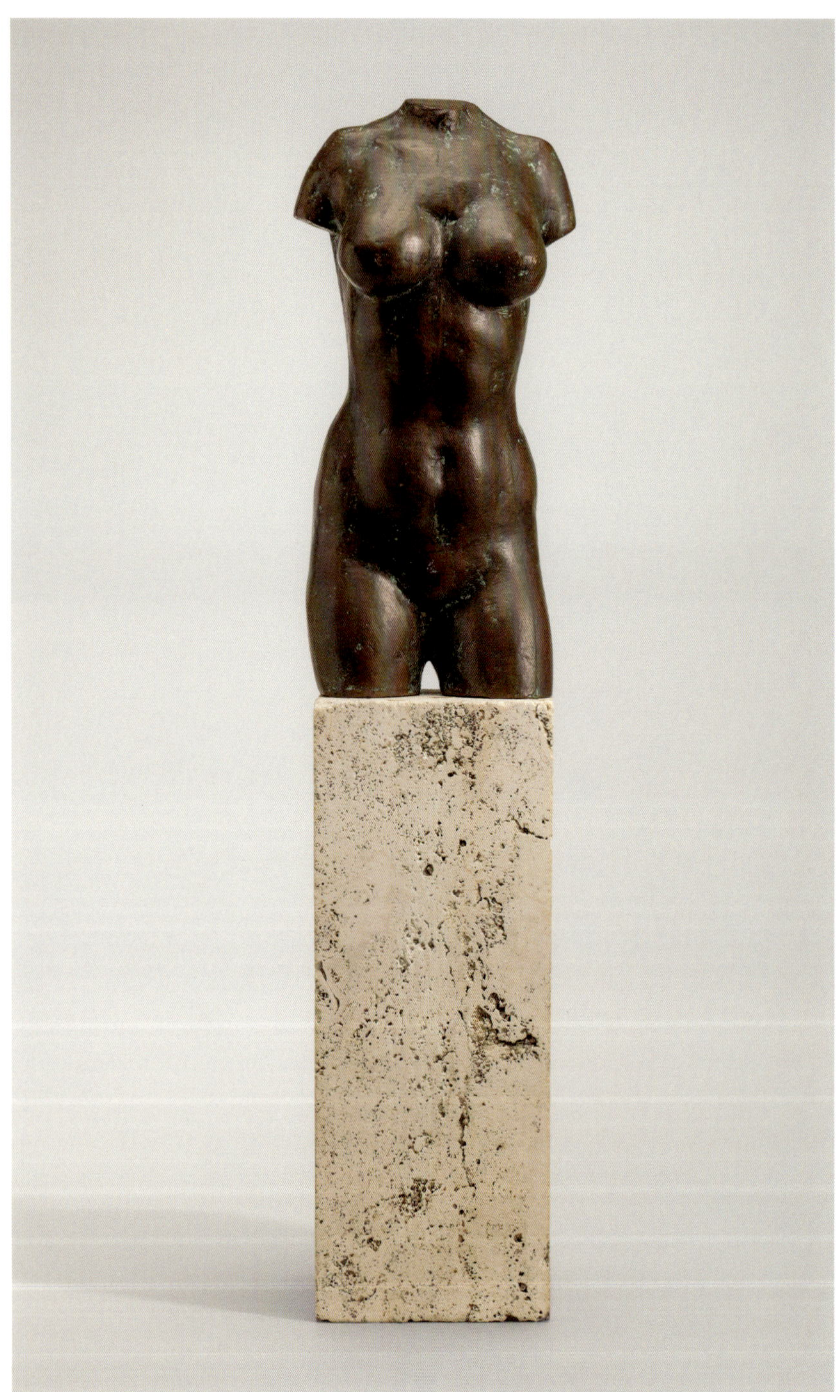

Marcel Guguianu, *Nude* (cat. 11)

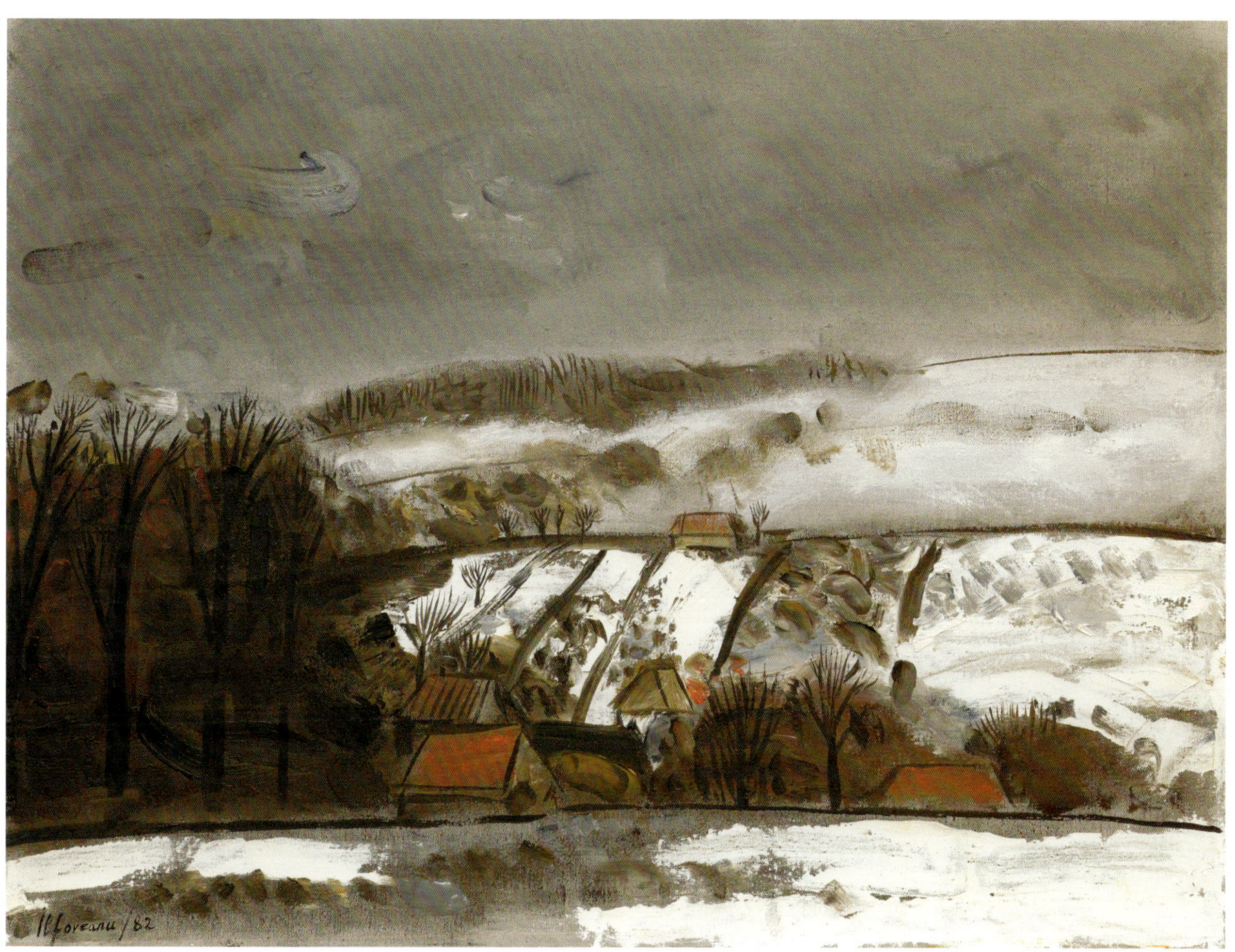

Sorin Ilfoveanu, *Iarna la Tescani* (cat. 12)

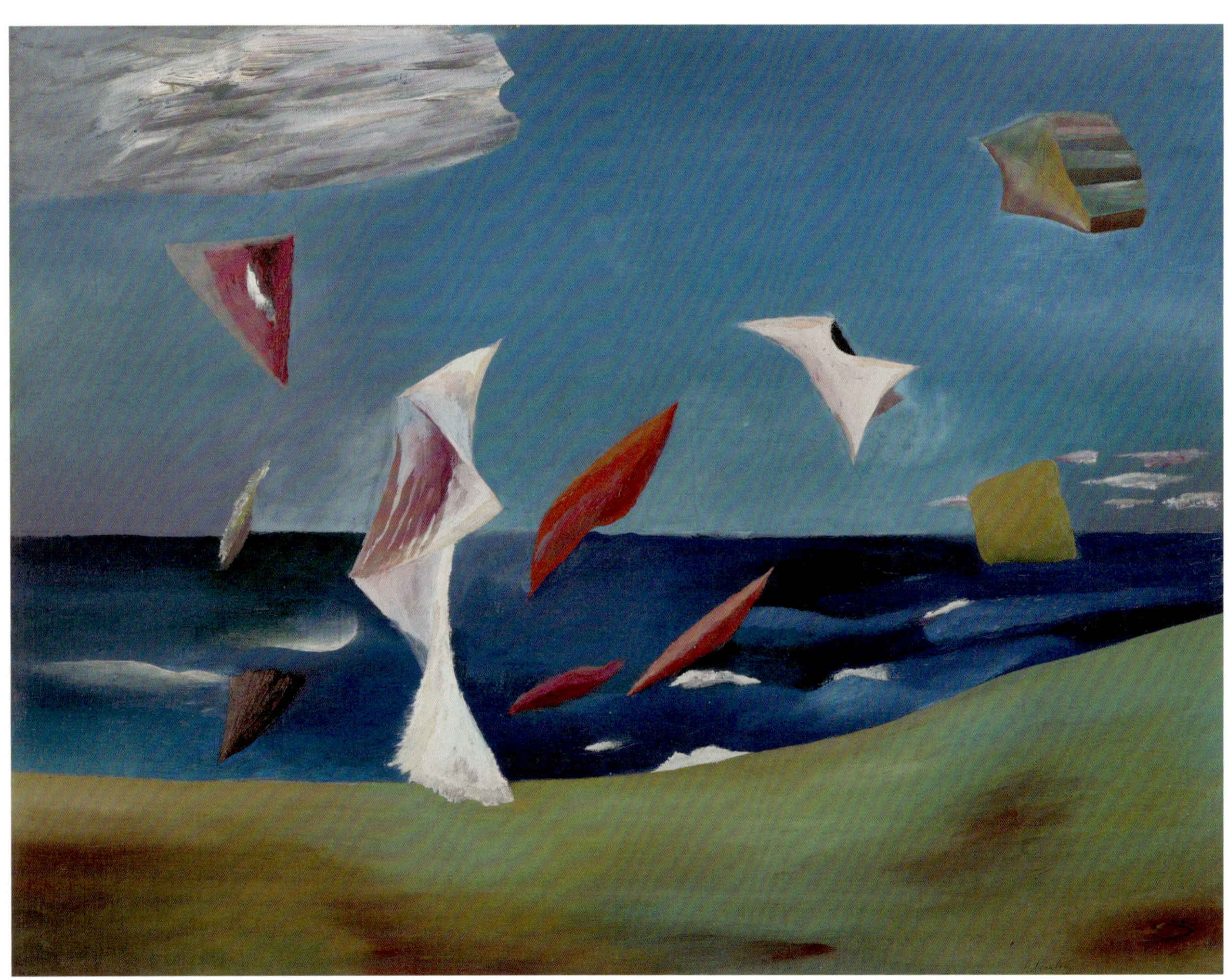

Ion Nicodim, *Surreal Sea* (cat. 14)

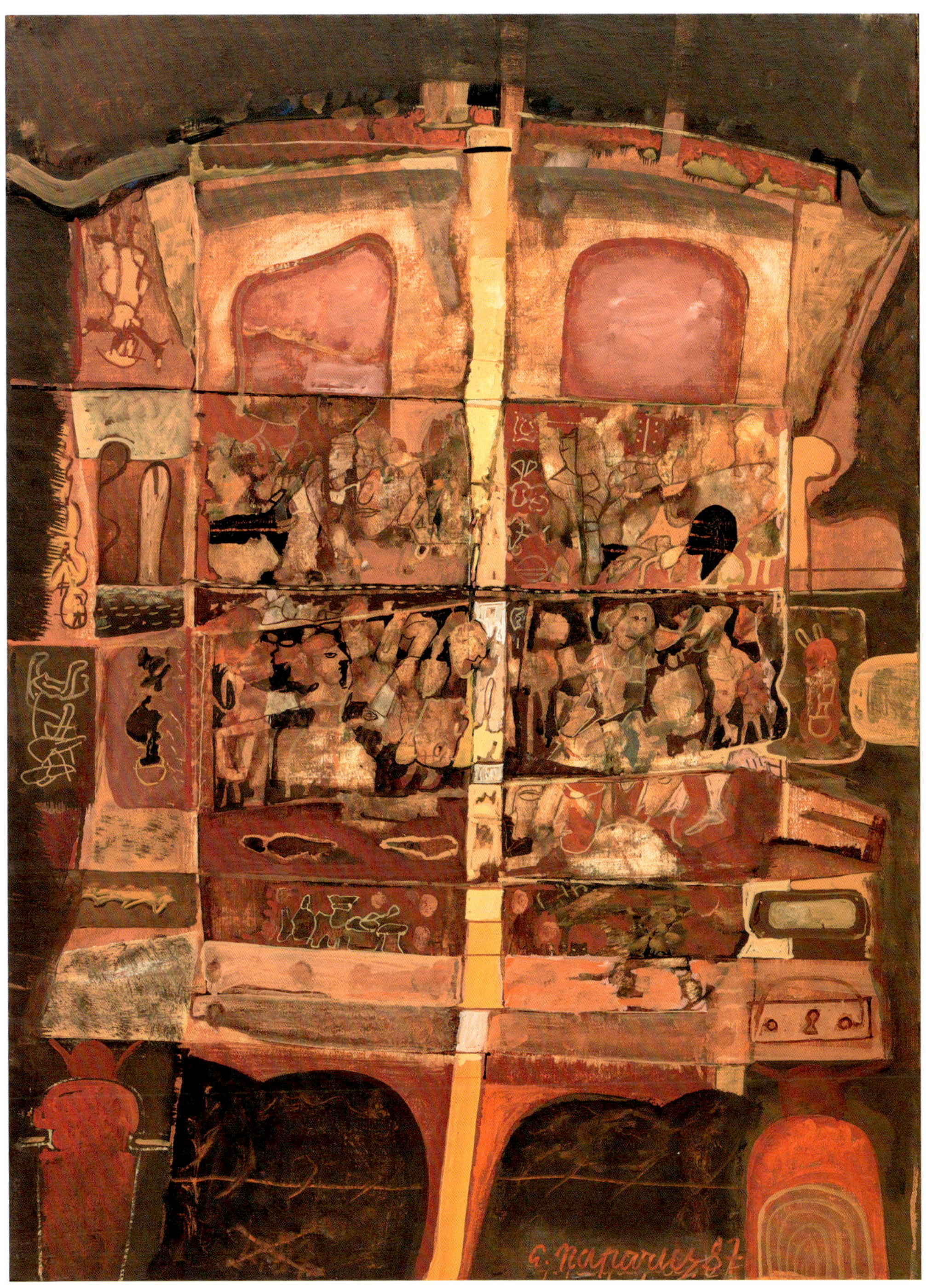

Georgeta Năpăruş, *Japanese Bureau* (cat. 13)

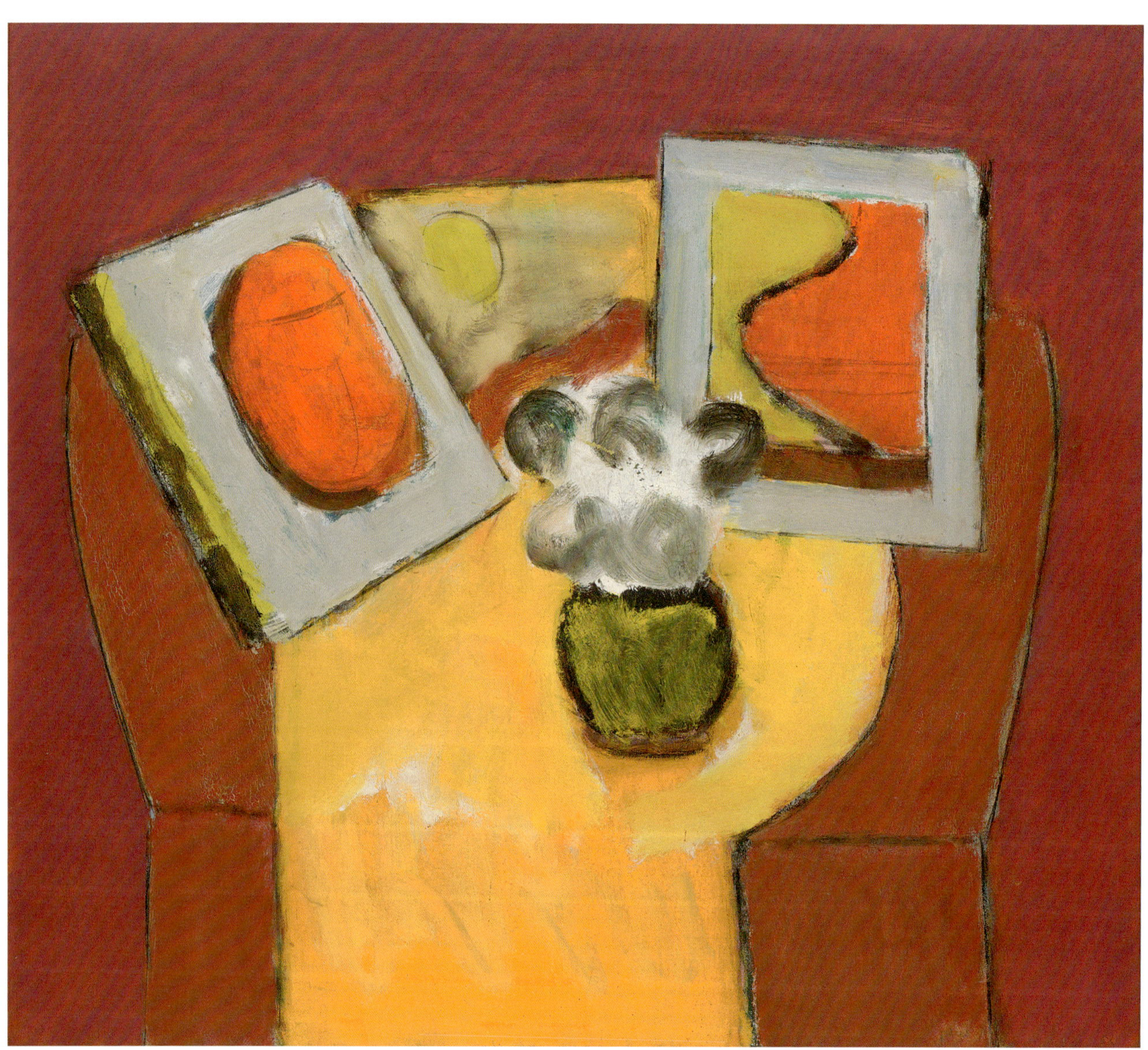

Ion Pacea, *Still Life on Table (Red Backgound)* (cat. 15)

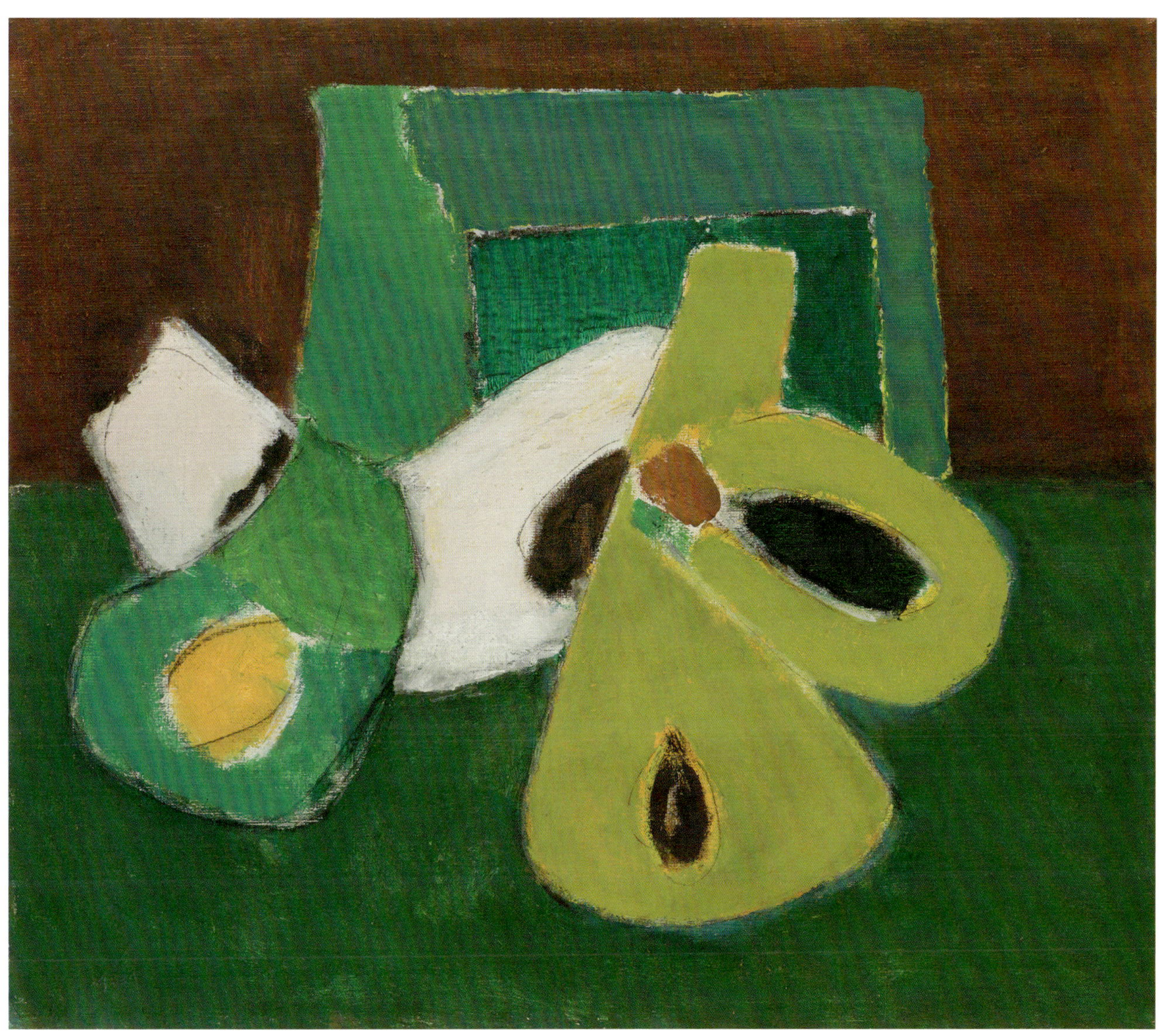

Ion Pacea, *Still Life on Table (with Green Forms)* (cat. 16)

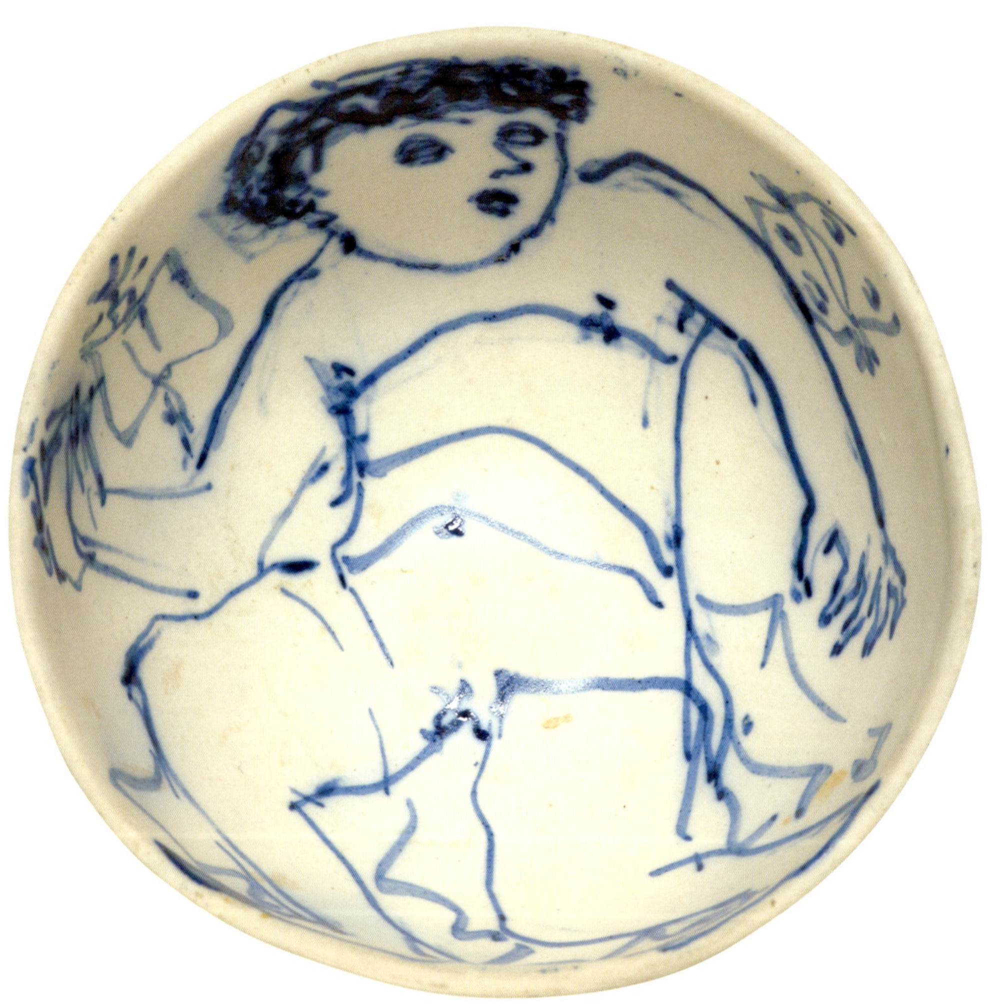

Silvia Radu, *Small Bowl* (cat. 65)

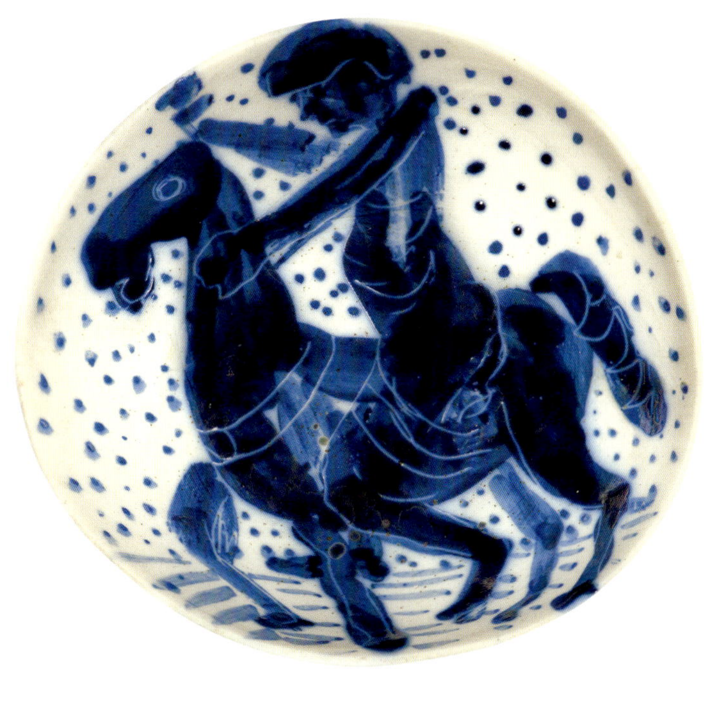

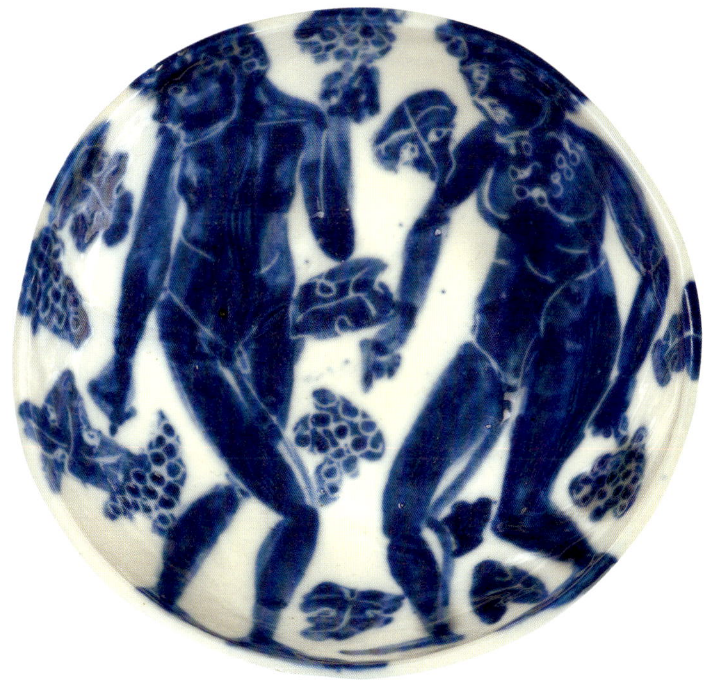

Silvia Radu, *Flat Bowls* (cats. 69 and 72)

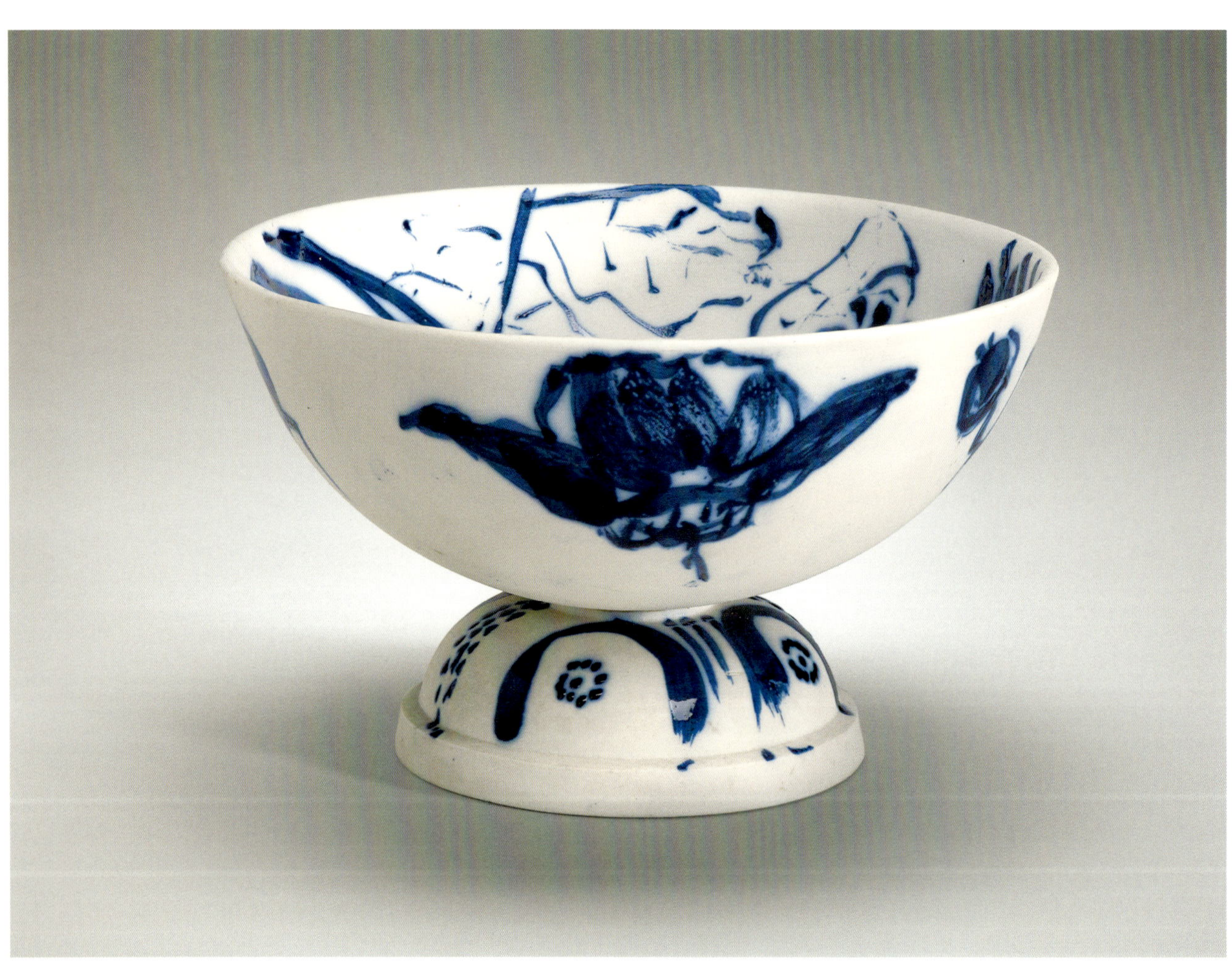

Silvia Radu, *Bowl with Stand* (cat. 74)

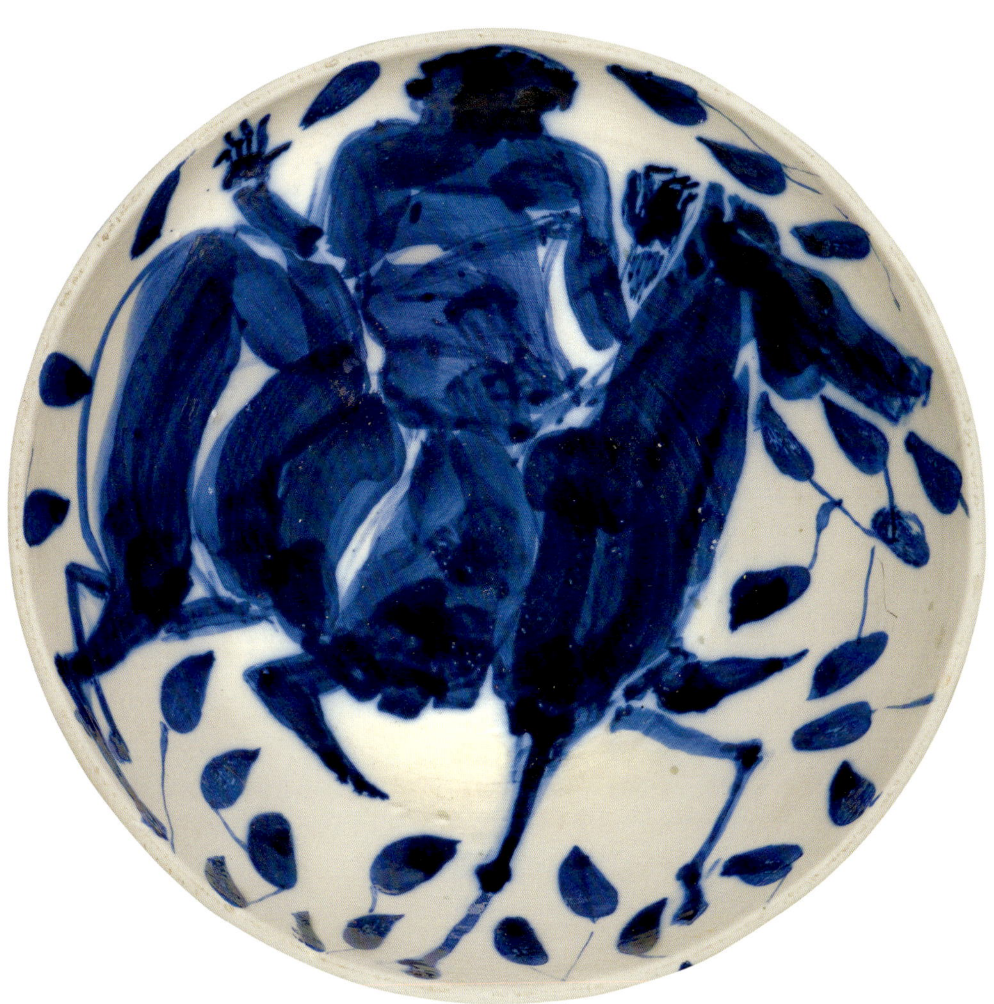

Silvia Radu, *Large Bowl* (cat. 76)

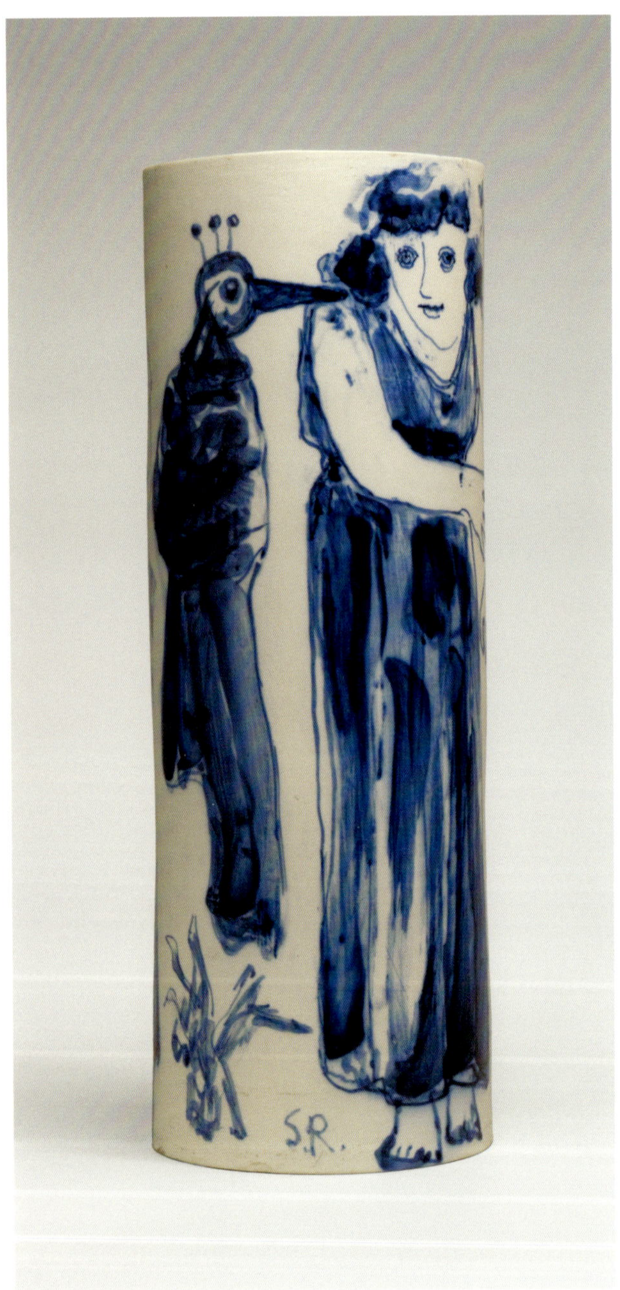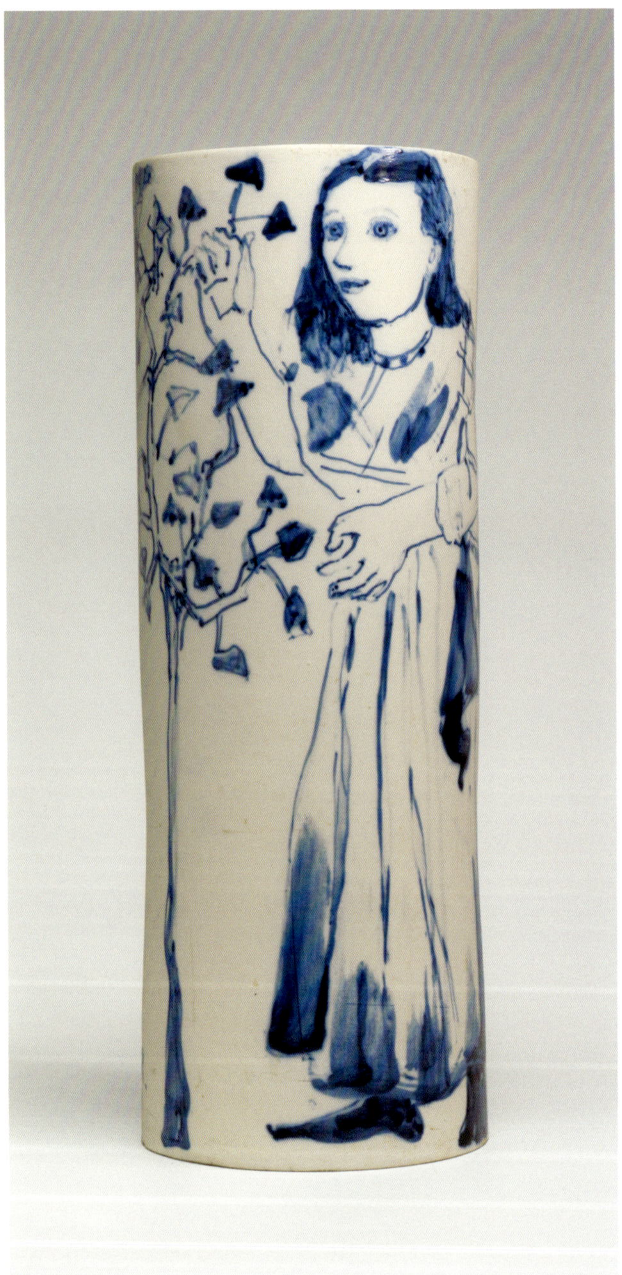

Silvia Radu, *Large Vase* (cat. 80)

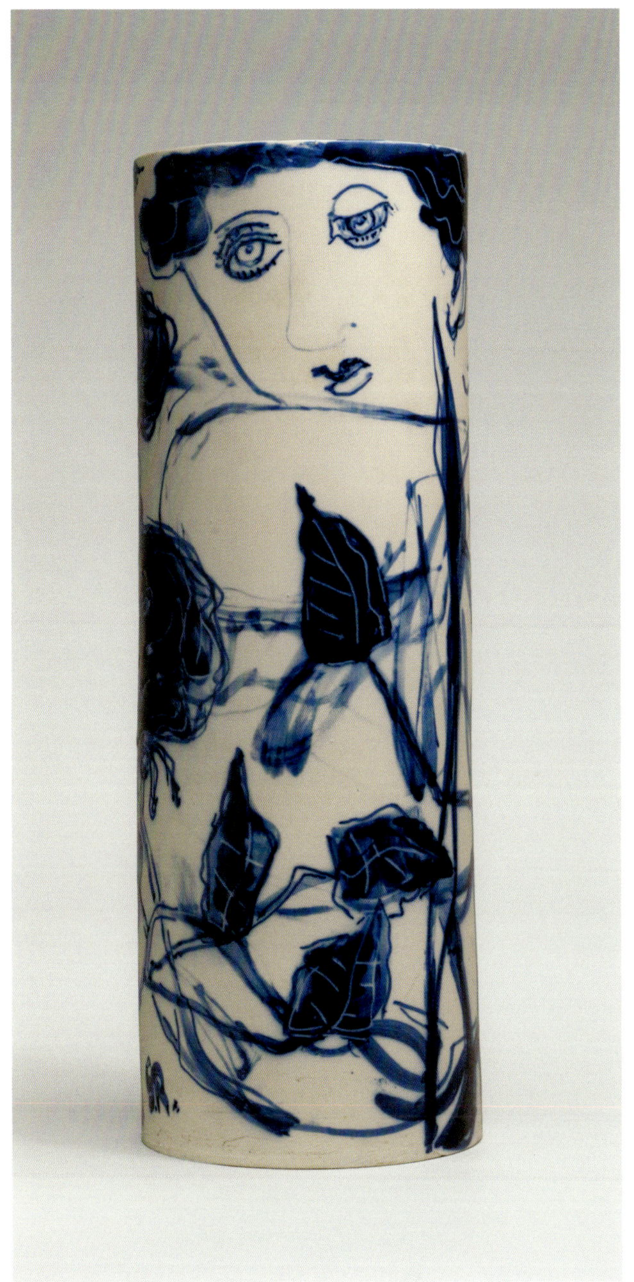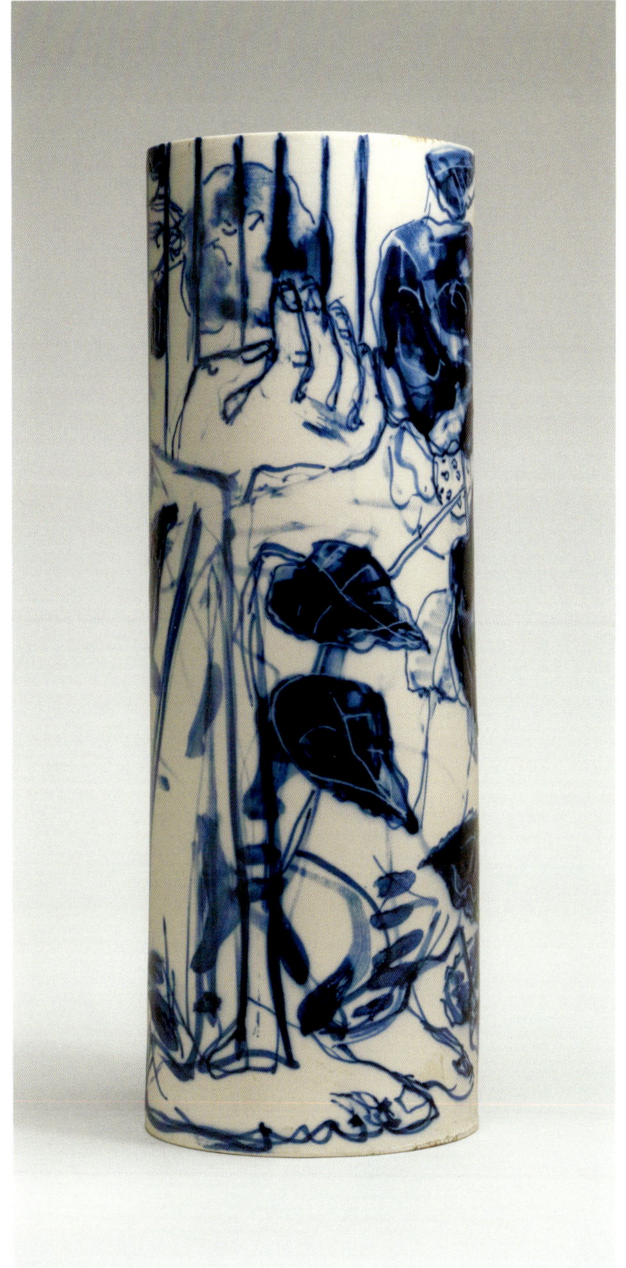

Silvia Radu, *Large Vase* (cat. 81)

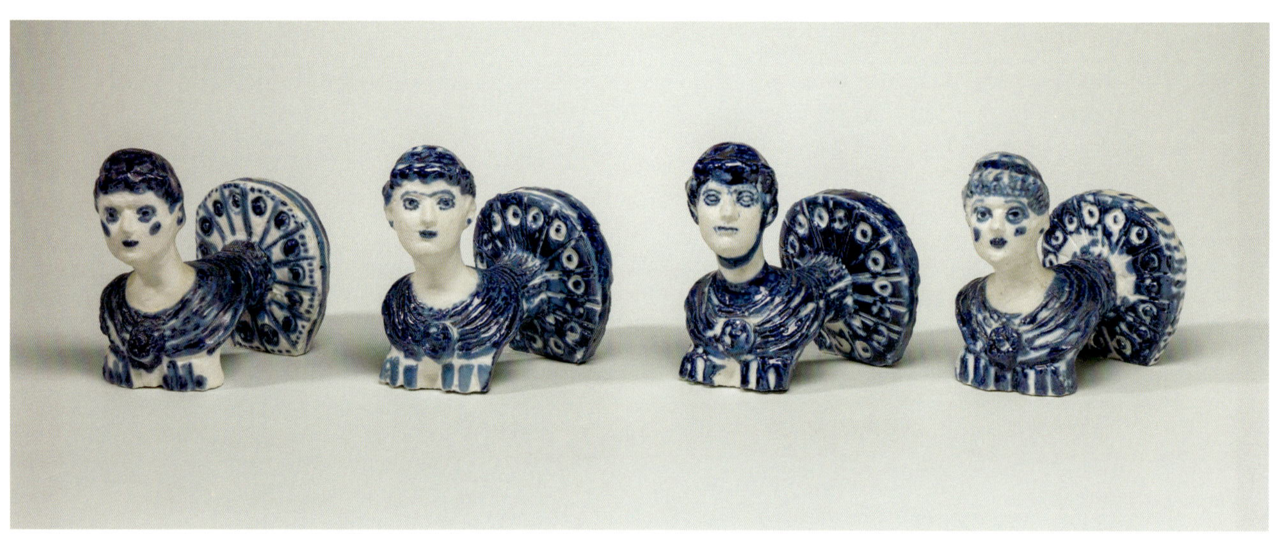

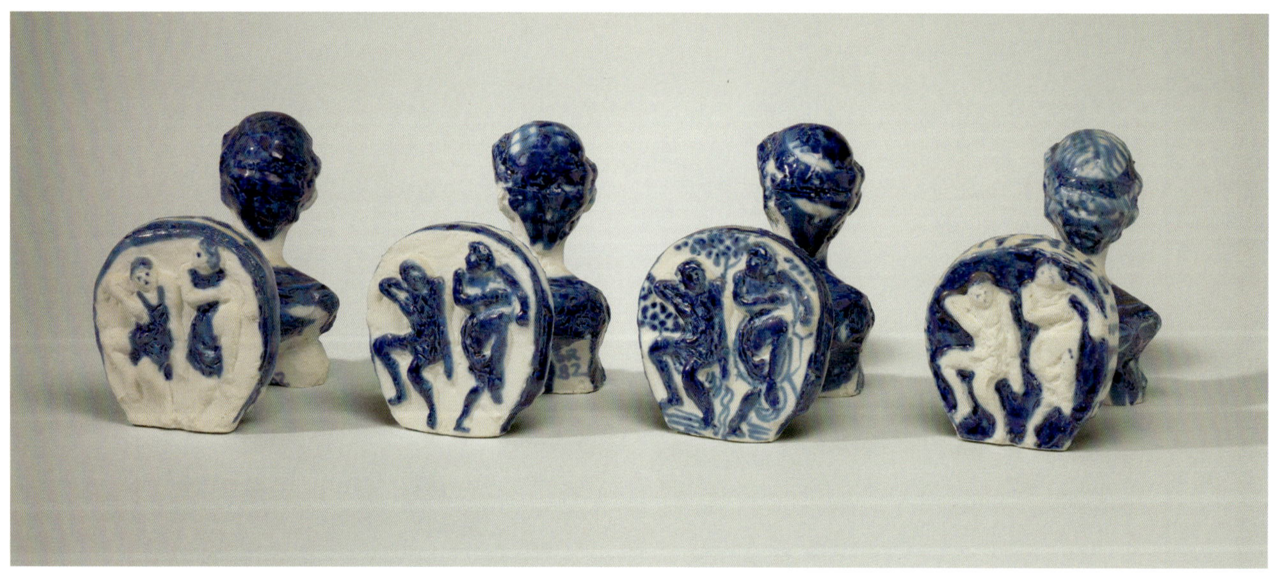

Silvia Radu, *Bookends* (cats. 83–86)

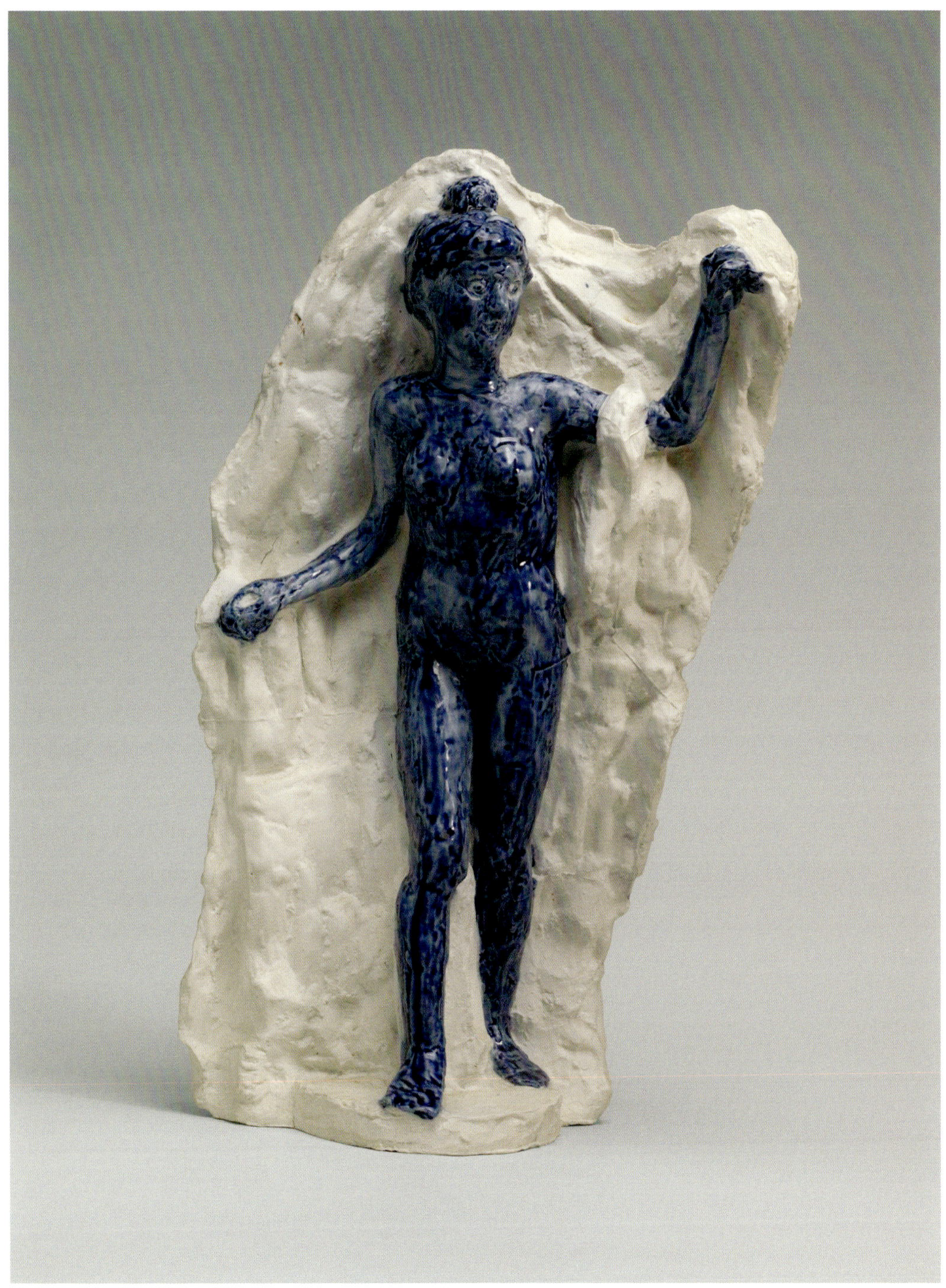

Silvia Radu, *Nude with Robe* (cat. 88)

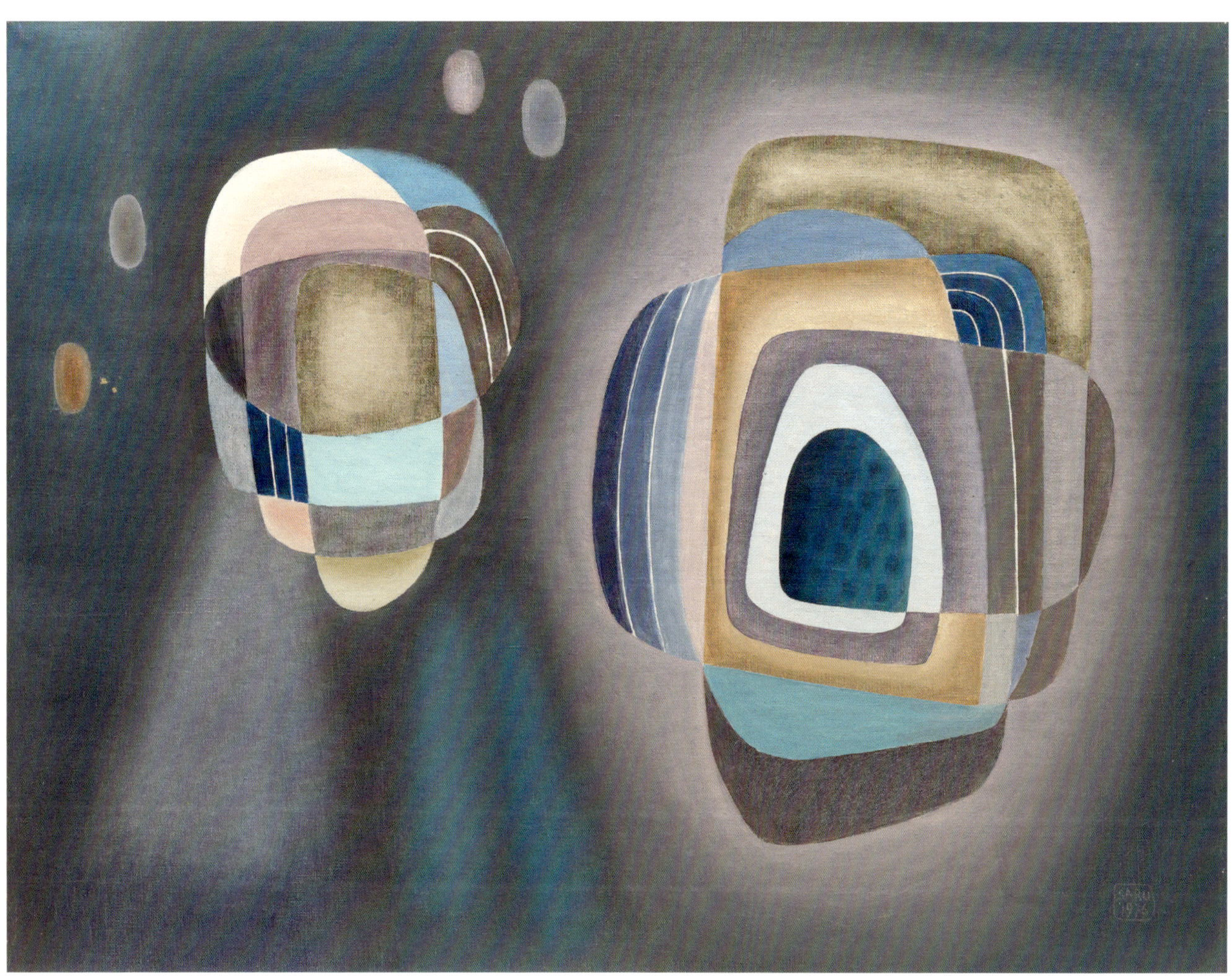

Gheorghe Şaru, *Forme in Spaţiu (Shapes in Space)* (cat. 90)

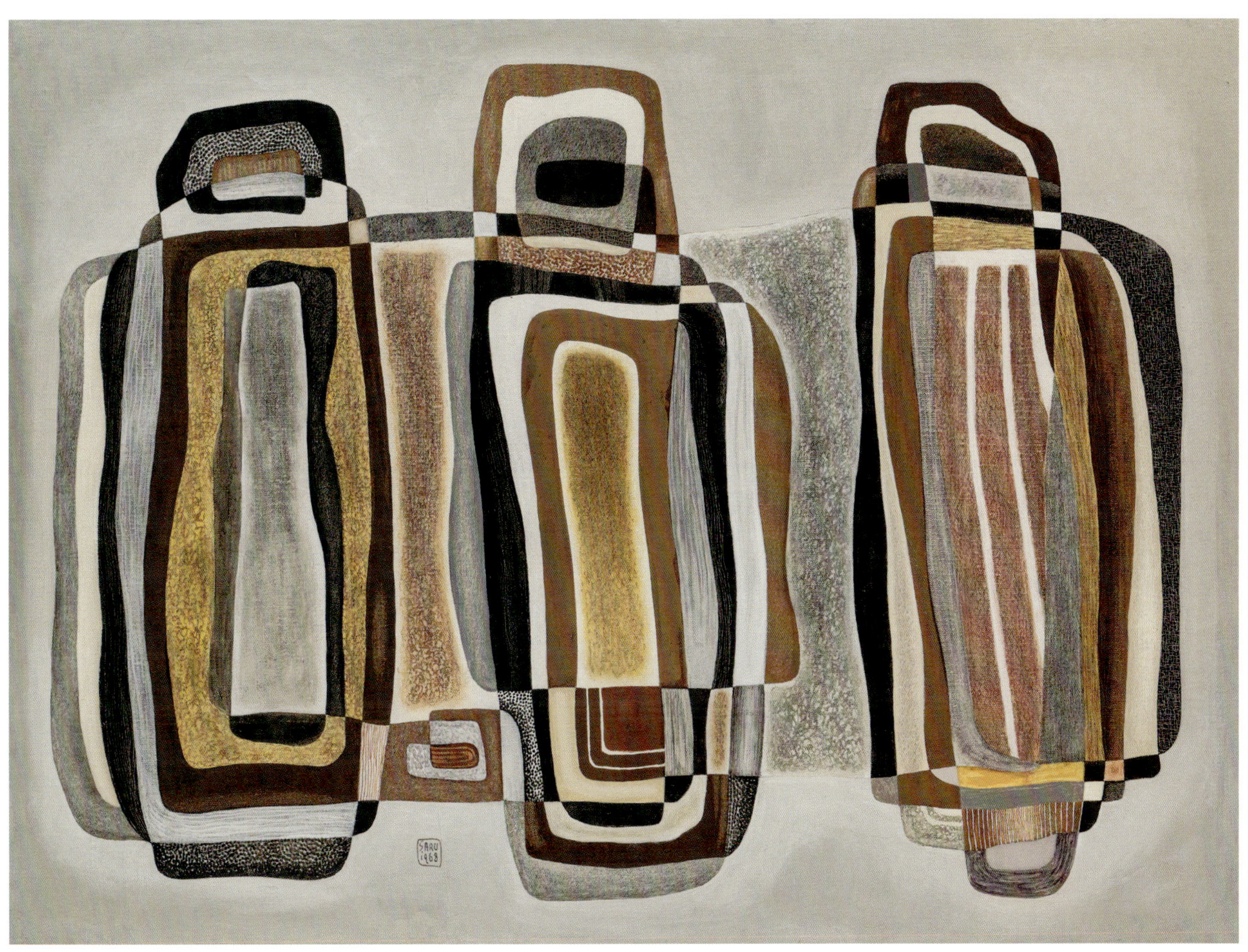

Gheorghe Şaru, *Untitled* (cat. 89)

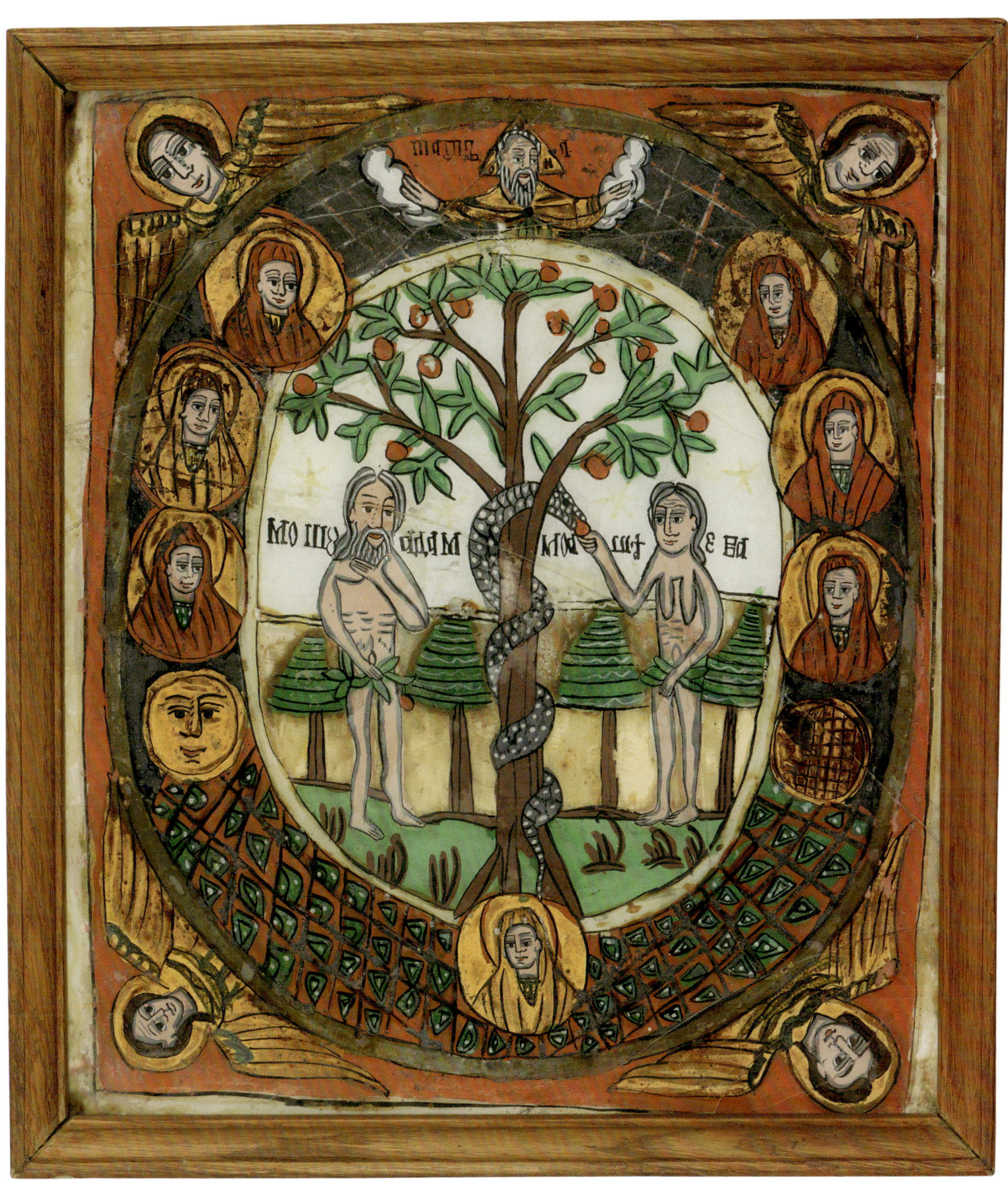

Icon Workshop, *Adam and Eve* (cat. 91)

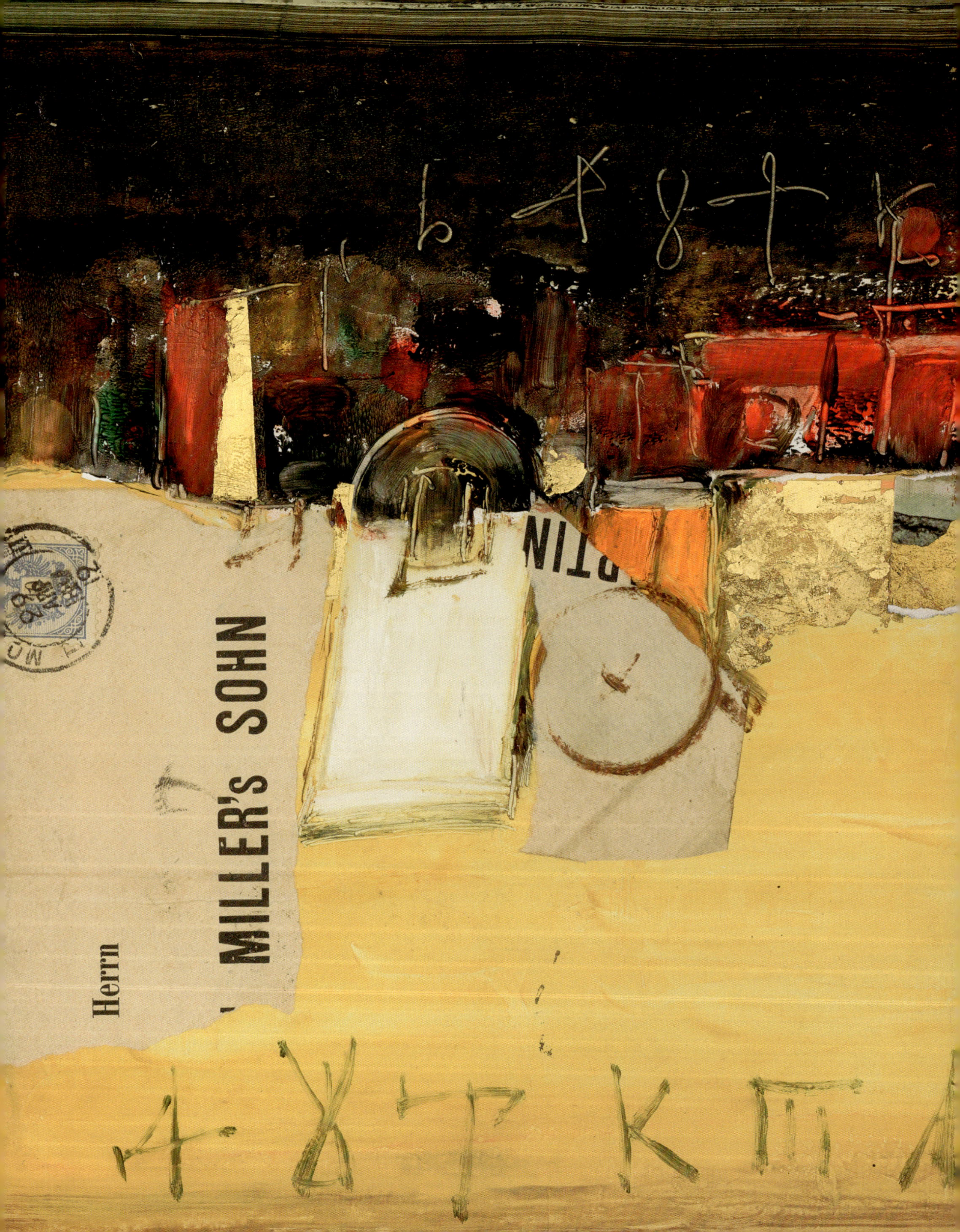

Herrn
MILLER's SOHN

Checklist of the Collection

This Checklist represents all of the artworks in my collection in Washington, DC — a small portion of the core collection at the University of Tasmania. The works' accession numbers identify them in the online Tyler Collection Research Repository maintained at UTAS: tylercollection.omeka.net

These works are listed alphabetically by their artists' surnames, and within that, chronologically as far as could be determined. The works' titles originated with their collector, Geoffrey, and were mostly adopted by Rachael Rose, Curator and Registrar at UTAS. In some cases — when the artist's own title has been discovered here on the work itself — I have updated it. These titles are often in Romanian.

Unframing the paintings and collages for their photography here has sometimes brought more information to light, revealing inscriptions that had been hidden behind the frames. An effort has been made to transcribe this.

The dimensions are of these artworks as unframed, in centimeters and inches, height before width, and including a third measurement for sculpture and ceramics.

Horia Bernea, 1938–2000

1. *Study for "Hill V"*
1976, oil on canvas, 25.4 × 75.6 cm
(10 × 29¾ in.), UTT 2017/056

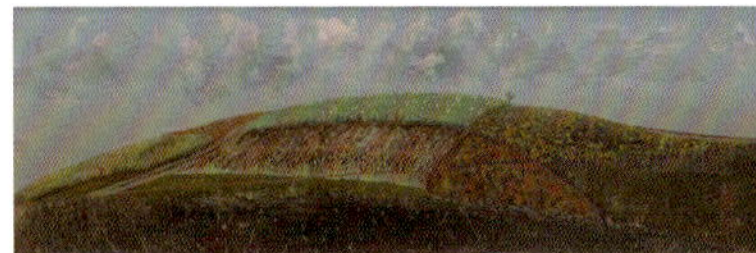

Inscriptions, lower right: "HB". Verso: "Horia Bernea — A Study for "Hill V" — medium Venetian 1976"

Horia Bernea, "who died not so old," Geoffrey recalled in a letter to Mariana, "was a good friend of the Gorduz and they gave me a number of small studies, mostly on paper, to add to the painting of his hill series that I bought from him after an introduction from Silvia."[1] The Gorduz also owned a "Hill" painting "which you used to have and which I hope still have in the bedroom at the studio — with a small damage!! — and of which I have a much smaller one that I bought at his studio through your introduction."[2]

(Plate illustration on page 45)

Ştefan Câlţia, born 1942

2. *Bărbat in Spectacol (Man in a Show)*
1975, oil on board, 33 × 27.6 cm (13 × 10⅞ in.), UTT 2017/064

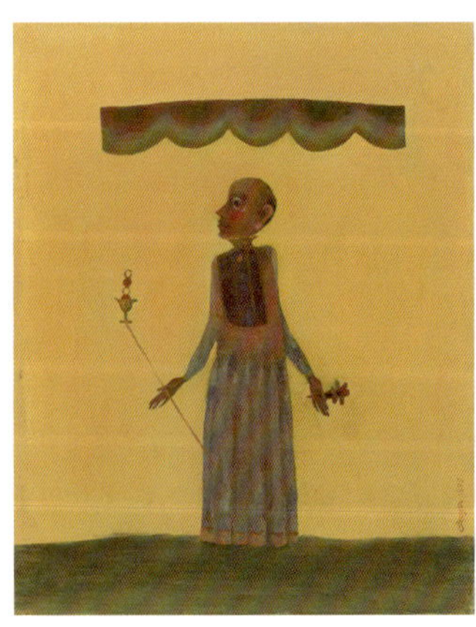

Inscriptions, right side edge: "CÂLŢIA 1975". Verso: "CALŢIA STEFAN / MAN IN A SHOW CENTER [illegible] / 'BĂRBAT IN SPECTACOL' ULEI PE LEMN 1975 26/32, 5 / STR. COLŢEI NR 14 / BUCUREŞT"

Geoffrey bought this, his first painting by Câlţia, at Fondul Plastic, "not knowing anything about the artist at all. It just looked to be a good painting.... It is in the best meticulously painted Caltia style, slightly in his fantastique manner but not excessively so.... it began my small collection of Caltia works."[3]

(Plate illustration on page 49)

3. *Toămna (Autumn)*
1980, oil on board, 49.7 × 49.7 cm
(19⅞ × 19⅞ in.), UTT 2017/066

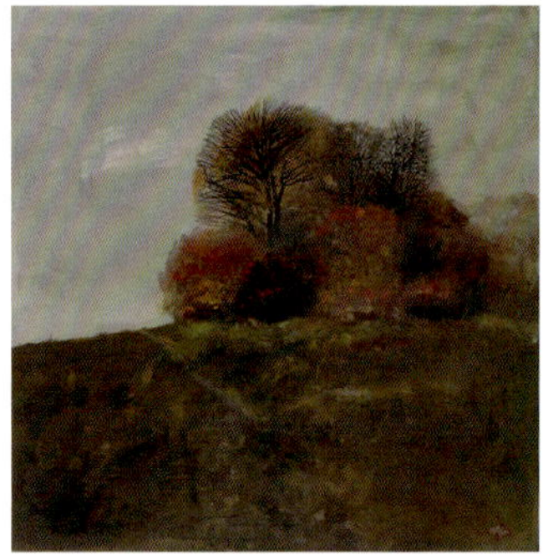

Inscriptions, lower right: "CALŢIA" [graphic]. Verso: "Câltia Stefan 'Toamnă' [*sic*] ulei pe carton + pînză 50/50 1980"

In a letter to the Petrescus, Geoffrey wrote, "There is a very fine landscape of a tree in a forest that you gave me." At Corneliu's suggestion, Geoffrey also bought other types of works by Câlţia, including "very fine pen and ink drawings" and "a book consisting of 25 etchings in his most fantastique manner; he gave me one of the copper plates from these works."[4]

4. *Cottage and Bird*
1982 (?), oil on board, 41.3 × 46 cm
(16¼ × 18⅛ in.), UTT 2017/065

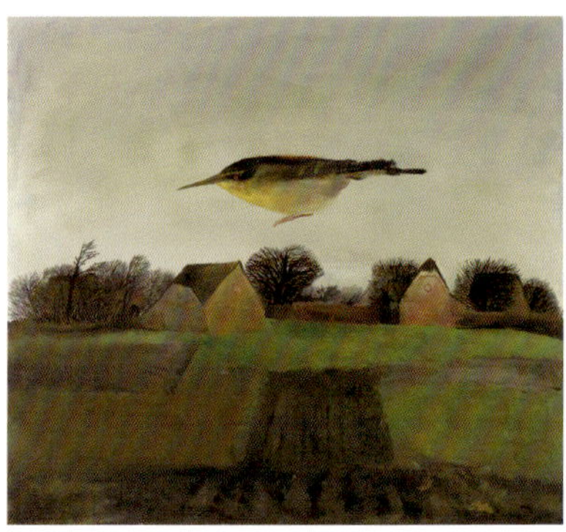

Inscriptions, lower right: "CÂLTIA 82 ?" [graphic]. Verso label: "TITLUL SAT [illegible] CU PASĂRE / TEHNICA ULEI [illegible] / AUTOR: ŞTEFAN CÂLŢIA / Bd. REPUBLICII Nr. 50 etaj 3 / BUCUREŞTI — ROMÂNIA / Telefon: 55.41.55 [with other faded writing]"

(Plate illustration on page 48)

Marin Gherasim, 1937–2017

5. *Poărta Jertfelor (Gate of the Sacrifices)*
1979, oil on linen, 64.8 × 60.3 cm
(25½ × 23¾ in.), UTT 2017/076

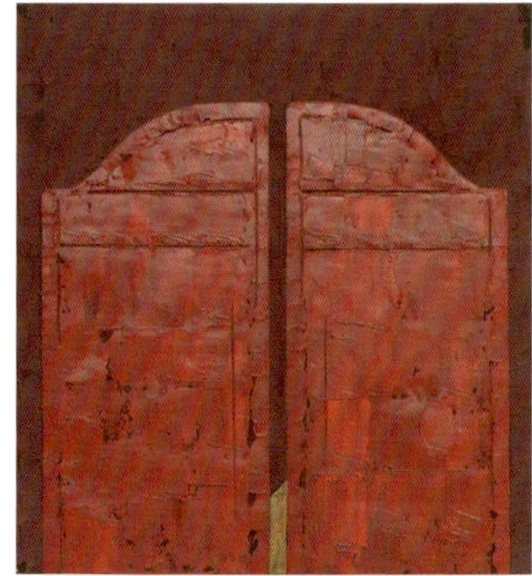

Inscriptions, center: "MG 79". Verso: "Marin Gherasim 'Poanta Jentfelon' [*sic*] 1979". On label: "No. 17 Mannheim 79 / Marin GHERASIM / Das Opfer Tor / Poerta jertfelor / O/L"

Gherasim was a member of the Group of 9 + 1, founded in 1981, which also included painters Horia Bernea (cat. 1), Florin Ciubotaru, Sorin Dumitrescu, and Horea Mihai; sculptors Doru Covrig, Vasile Gorduz (cats. 6–10), Bata Marianov, Napoleon Tiron; and art critic Andrei Pleşu.

The label indicates — and art historian Éduard Andrei confirms — that this work was exhibited in a group exhibition in Mannheim, Germany, in 1979. A stamp on the verso is likely from a Romanian official office authorizing the export of this work. The same stamp appears on the verso on several other artworks.

(Plate illustration on page 51)

Vasile Gorduz, 1931–2008

6. *Ordinary Bird (Bird Sleeping)*
Undated, stone, 18.4 × 15.2 × 10.2 cm
(7¼ × 6 × 4 in.) variable, UTT 2017/096

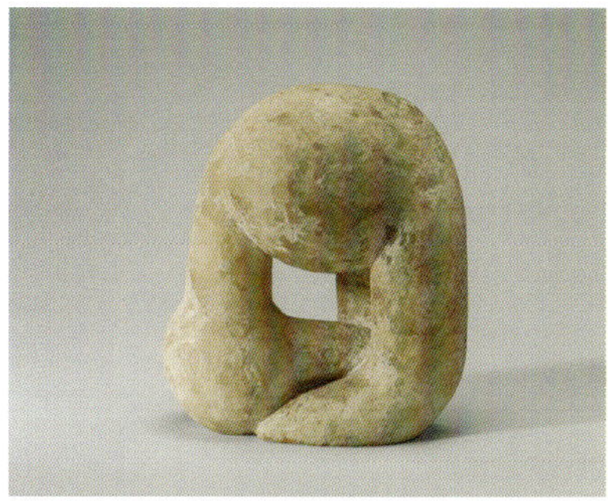

Gorduz returned again and again to his "ordinary bird" sculptures, always in this same evocative posture, in stone and bronze and in varying heights. Geoffrey collected several. Sorin Dumitrescu, who also noted an influence of Brancusi, saw here a riddle, a profound "mystery of … a bird nesting in its own shape."[5] Geoffrey recalled that this "bird asleep" was done by Gorduz "at the seaside from rocks that he found."[6]

(Plate illustration on page 52)

7. *Portrait of Geoffrey Tyler*
Undated, bronze, 35.6 × 29.9 × 21.6 cm
(14 × 11¾ × 8½ in.) variable,
UTT 2017/098

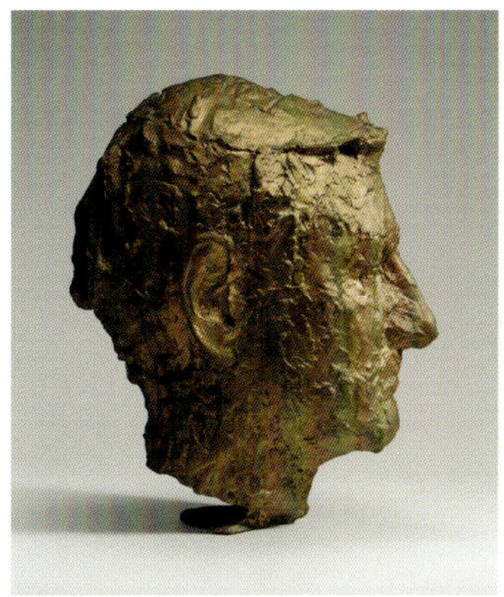

Geoffrey would sit for Gorduz on his visits to Bucharest. The clay model was done over a period of at least three years. Between visits, Gorduz buried the bust in his garden to keep the clay from drying out, but at one point he couldn't remember where he had buried it. It is also possible that his wife mischievously had moved it. "Then he was not able to get bronze to make the casting," he wrote to Mariana. "Eventually it was finished about five years after he gave me the first sitting."[7] Neither artist nor sitter was completely satisfied with the final effort. Geoffrey wrote, "It makes me look much more handsome than I deserve!"[8]

To Silvia, the artist's wife, Geoffrey wrote, "I shall always remember Vasile in the studio, sitting and talking, sculpting my 'head' and in the garden tending his beloved vines"[9] — from which he produced a robust red wine.

(Plate illustration on page 7)

8. *Bird Swallowing Its Own Shadow*
Undated, bronze, 38.1 × 23.5 × 15.6 cm
(15 × 9¼ × 6¼ in.) variable, UTT 2017/097

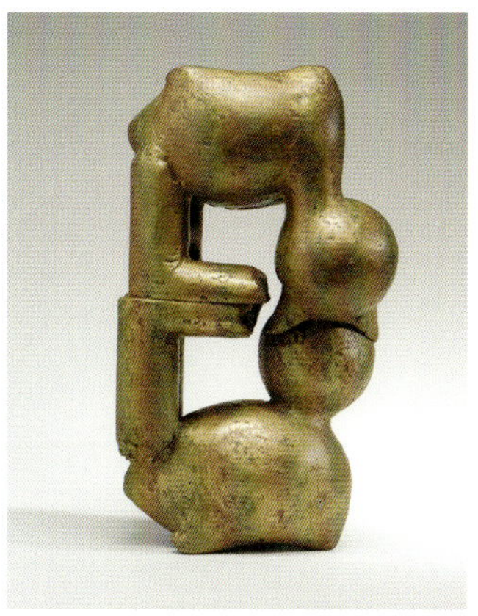

Inscriptions, at one end: "Vama 1985". At the other end: "Gorduz" in characteristic graphic signature

Some of Gorduz's work followed "ancient Egyptian footsteps," wrote Romanian art critic Dan Hăulică — musing that a bird "crouches in the depths of its self, into Mallarmean misflights which have failed to break free from their crust."[10]

The inscriptions at both ends of the piece pose the riddle of how to install it.

(Plate illustration on page 53)

9. *Abstract*
Undated, bronze, 12 × 9.5 × 6.4 cm
(4¾ × 3¾ × 2½ in.) variable, UTT 2017/100

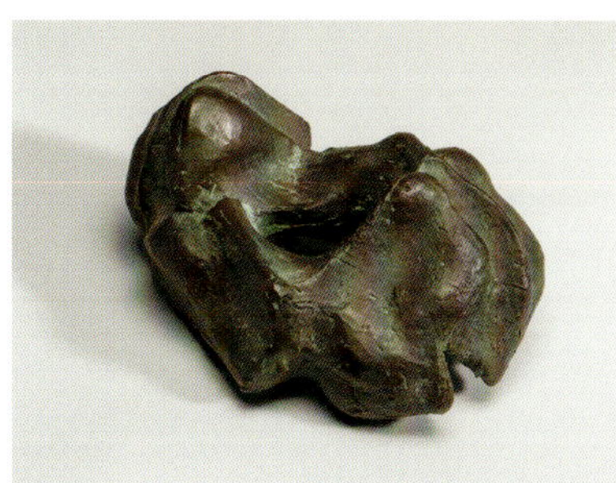

10. *Horse head*
Undated, bronze, 16.5 × 17.8 × 7.3 cm
(6½ × 7 × 2⅞ in.) variable, UTT 2017/099

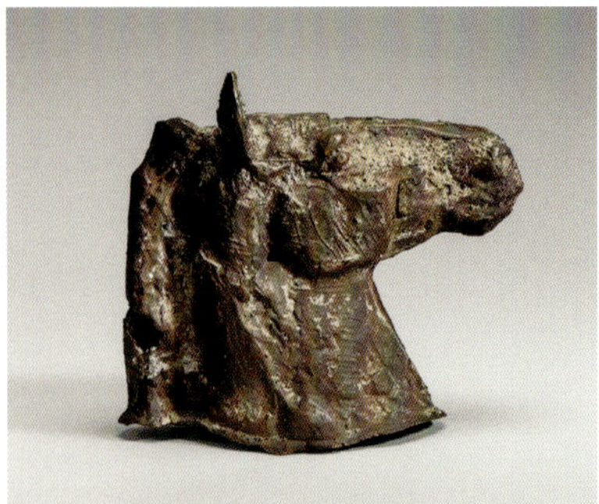

Geoffrey liked this "faulty casting of a horse's head which I like more with its fault than I would if it were a perfect casting."[11]

Marcel Guguianu, 1922–2012

11. *Nude*
Undated, bronze and stone,
49.5 × 10.2 × 8.6 cm (19½ × 4 × 3⅜ in.)
variable, UTT 2017/092

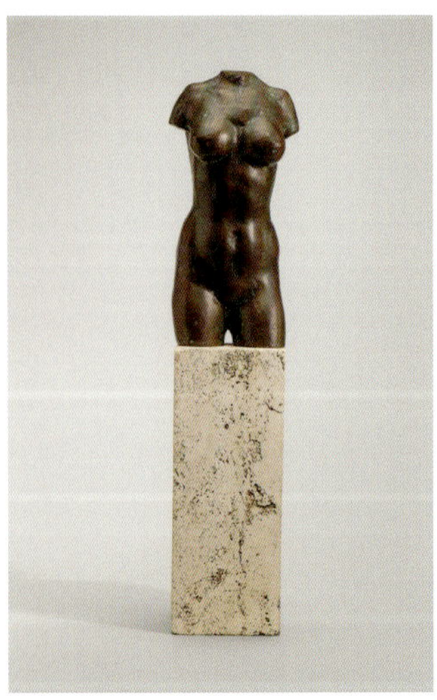

Geoffrey had bought this work at Fondul Plastic but could only remember that the artist was a friend of the Gorduz. He wrote to Petrescu asking for help — which Petrescu was able to give.

(Plate illustration on page 54)

Sorin Ilfoveanu, born 1946

12. *Iarna la Tescani*
1982, oil on canvas, 55.2 × 73.7 cm
(21¾ × 29 in.), UTT 2017/040

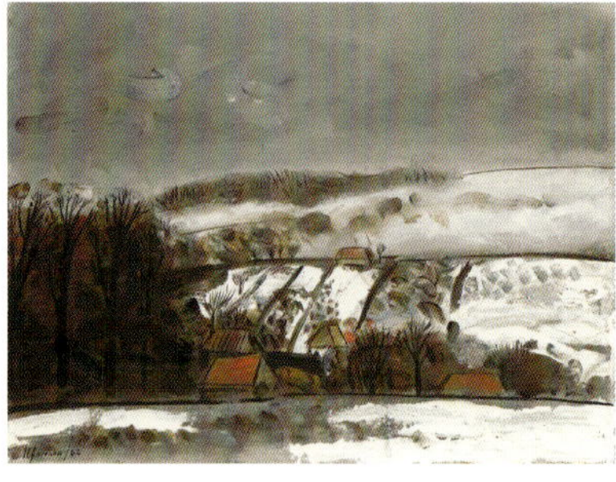

Inscriptions, lower left: "Ilfoveanu/82". Verso: "Ilfoveanu/82 'Iarna la Tescani' ulei panza 55 × 75"

Tescani is a village in Moldavia, in north-eastern Romania.

I had the good fortune to visit Ilfoveanu in his studio in 2018, to which I owe Anamaria Maior for introducing us. This was eye-opening: since the early 1980s, Ilfoveanu's art has taken a dramatically new direction.

(Plate illustration on page 55)

Georgeta Năpăruş, 1930–1997

13. *Japanese Bureau*
1987, oil on canvas, 72.7 × 54 cm
(28⅝ × 21¼ in.), UTT 2017/075

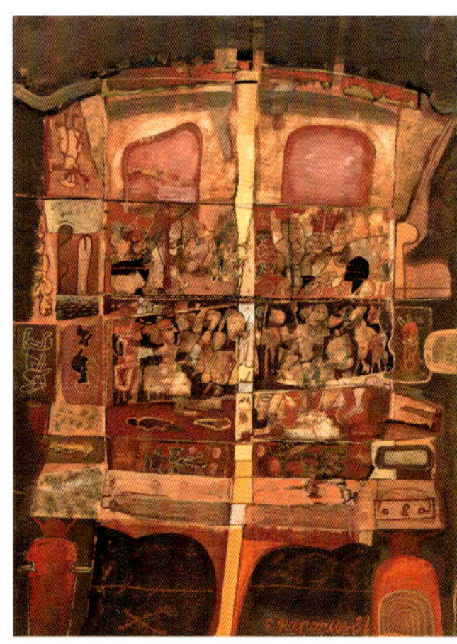

Inscriptions, lower right: "G Naparus 87". Verso: "'la petit [*sic*] armoire japonais Georgeta NAPARUS (ulei pe pinza) executed 1987 Bucuresti Romania"

On a visit to Năpăruş's son, Ilie, in Florida, we saw the Japanese bureau that is the subject of this painting.

Năpăruş's work was much sought-after. It was "always difficult to buy from her, since she never had much for sale. . . . I cannot ever remember having seen a Naparus or a Grigorescu in any of the galleries. I suppose it must have been that they were able to sell almost everything as soon as it was painted."[12]

Geoffrey did succeed, however, in buying a number of works by the artist and her husband, Octav Grigorescu.

(Plate illustration on page 57)

Ion Nicodim, 1932–2007

14. *Surreal Sea*
Undated, oil on board, 39.4 × 50.2 cm
(15½ × 19¾ in.), UTT 2017/070

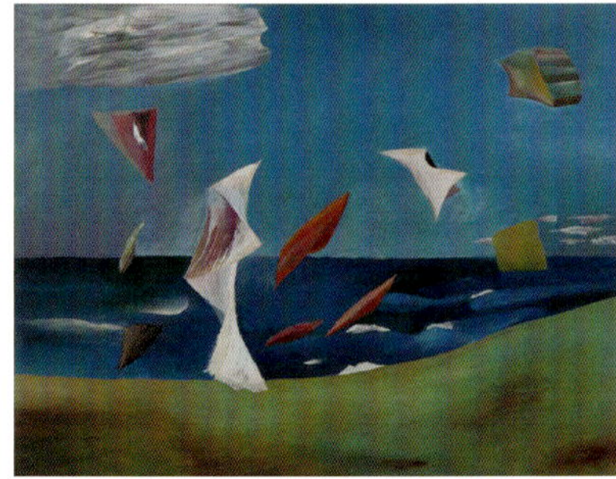

Inscription on stretcher: "Ion Nicodim"

To Petrescu, Geoffrey wrote that although he never met Nicodim, "you gave me a painting that I think is by him. It is a surrealist seascape, very nice in a gold Romanian frame."[13]

(Plate illustration on page 56)

Ion Pacea, 1924–1999

15. *Still Life on Table (Red Background)*
Undated, oil on canvas, 79.4 × 90.2 cm
(31¼ × 35½ in.), UTT 2017/058

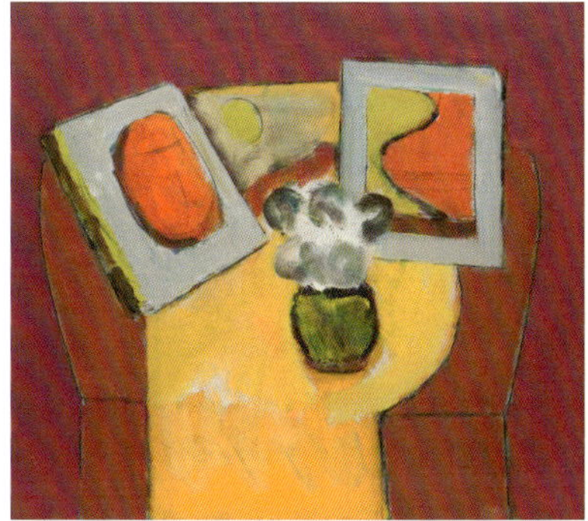

Inscription, lower right: "Pacea"

Writing to the Petrescus in February 2008, Geoffrey "was thinking of Pacea recently.... I have a number of his paintings and he is an artist whose works have grown in my mind the longer I have looked at them. I suppose he was much influenced by Matisse.... His paintings have the some [*sic*] simplicity together with lovely colours and they are always pleasant things to look at, as well as interesting. He was a nice man too....I usually spent a pleasant evening at his nice apartment with his wife and family.... Lucretia [*sic*; she was Lucrezia] ...was an artist in fabrics; she spoke good English as well as being a good cook. Their apartment was filled with beautiful things."[14] Most artists lived in much humbler circumstances.

(Plate illustration on page 58)

16. *Still Life on Table (with Green Forms)*
Undated, oil on canvas, 69.8 × 82.2 cm
(27½ × 32⅜ in.), UTT 2017/059

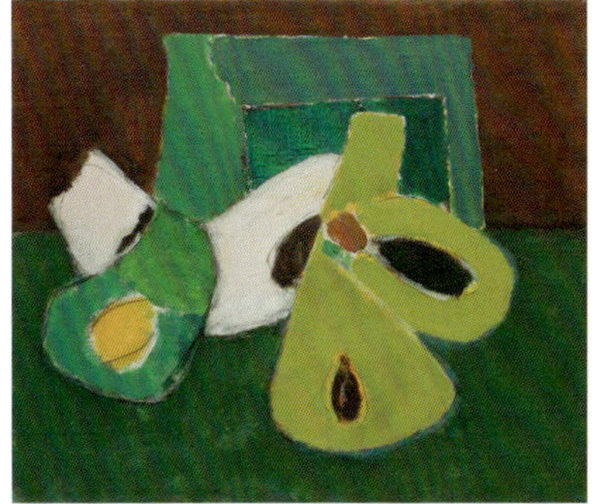

Inscription, lower left: "Pacea"

A painting virtually identical to this one is illustrated in *Ion Pacea: O Posibilă Retrospectivă* by Constantin Pacea. Titled *Interior cu plantă și para van I*, it is dated circa 1968, though Geoffrey believed that Pacea never dated his works.[15]

Gorduz made a bronze bust of Pacea — and also of Petrescu, Ion Gheorghiu, Octav Grigorescu (husband of Georgeta Năpăruș), and other artists.

(Plate illustration on page 59)

Corneliu Petrescu, 1924–2009

17. *Eastern Story*
1973, oil on paper, 40 × 48.9 cm
(15¾ × 19¼ in.), UTT 2017/082

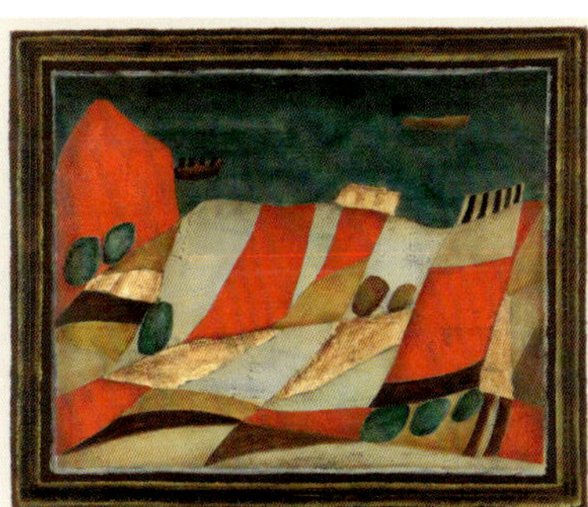

Inscriptions, lower right: "C Petrescu 73".
Verso: Label: "Uniunea Artistilor Plastici, Calea Victoriei Nr. 155 — Bucuresti / Romania / Nr. 13. / Autor: Corneliu Petrescu / Tutlul Lucrării: Eastern Story / Dimensuni: 40/49 cms / Technica: Mixed Media / Anul Execuției: / Preț"

This painting was hung in "the bottom room where I listen to music," Geoffrey wrote, "a realistic autumn Romanian landscape that Corneliu used on the cover of the catalogue of a Bucharest exhibition."[16]

18. *Angel in Sky*
1974, mixed media on artists' board,
14.9 × 21.3 cm (5⅞ × 8⅜ in.), UTT 2017/002

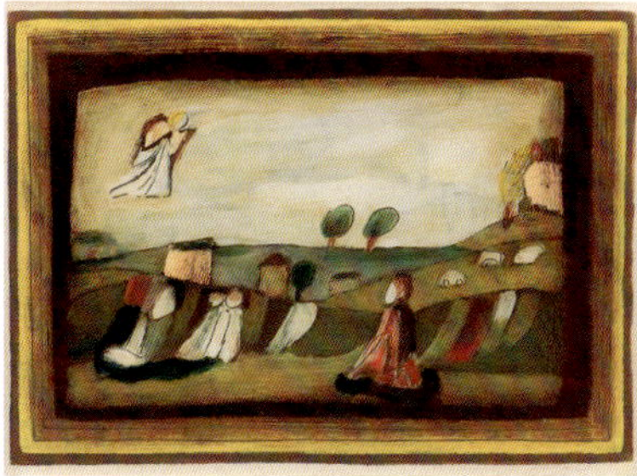

Inscriptions, lower right: "C. Petrescu". Verso (*illustrated on page 96*): "Bucharest / The 3rd of November 1974 / Dear Mr. Tyler, / It is a long time since I had no news from you — and during this period a lot of things happened ...But important was that my mother died — also ... / I began to paint new paintings for future exhibitions (when you will come in Bucharest you'll have the opportunity to see them) — Anyhow — I beg you — to be so kind — and to help me to have another exhibition there on the Spring 1976. / For Christmas and New Year — to you and your wife — the best wishes of health and happiness from my wife and me. / Corneliu"

(Plate illustration on page 25)

19. *Untitled*
1974, mixed media on artists' board,
23.5 × 18.7 cm (9¼ × 7⅜ in.), UTT 2017/045

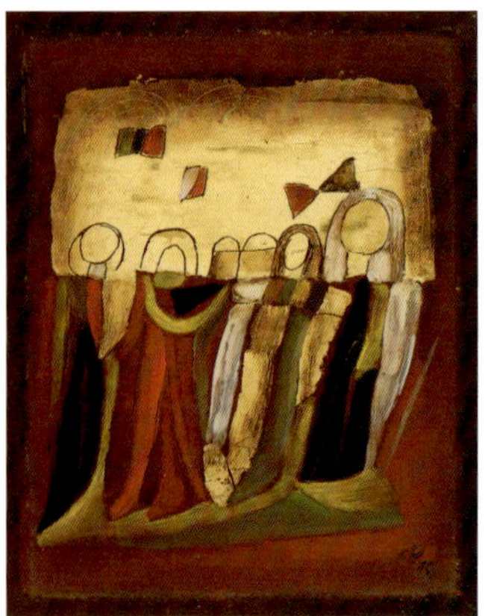

Inscription, lower right: "CP 74"

20. *Icon*
Mid-1970s, painted wood, 29.2 × 25.1 × 1.5 cm
(11½ × 9⅞ × ⅝ in.) variable, UTT 2017/009

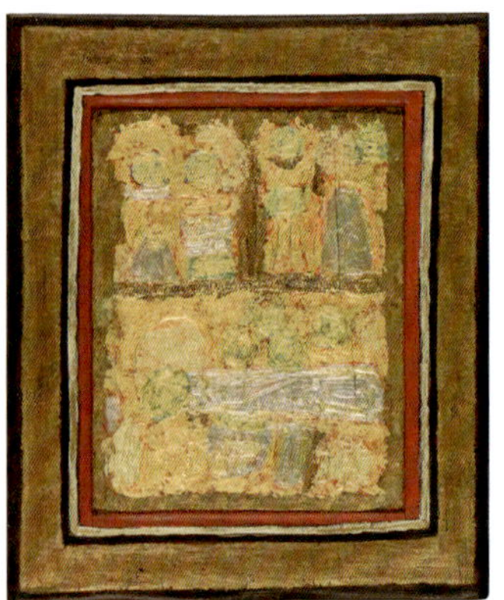

"Byzantium saturates the history of Romanian art," Geoffrey wrote in his essay about this pervasive influence on Petrescu. In Ceauşescu's time, "the communists could suffer religious art if it could be viewed as 'peoples art' and specifically 'Romanian'"—an ambivalence that allowed Petrescu "to incorporate religious themes and byzantine techniques into his works, without overt problems with the state." In this icon, the entombment of Christ

"takes up the bottom two thirds…with the top consisting of two highly stylized icon themes that are pure abstractions rather than recognisable as particular designs.…Rather they seem to be memories from Petrescu's mind of the concept of icon themes, dreams rather than waking recollections."[17]

21. *Angel*
Undated, painted wood, 24.8 × 15.6 × 2 cm
(9¾ × 6 × ¾ in.) variable, UTT 2017/010

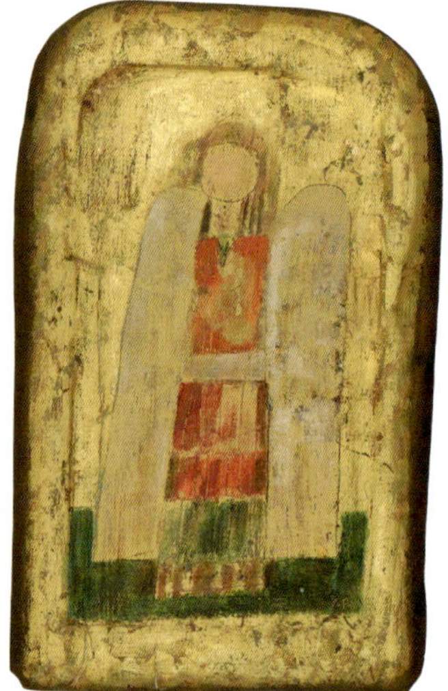

Inscription, lower right: "CP"

(Plate illustration on page 24)

22. *Self-Portrait*
1975, oil on paper, 32.4 × 32.4 cm
(12¾ × 12¾ in.), UTT 2017/071

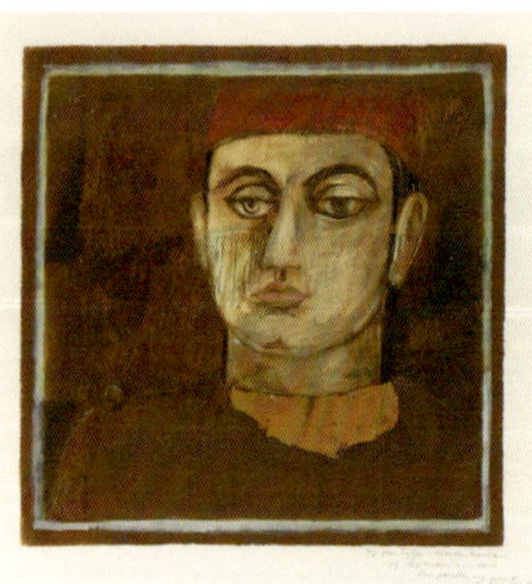

Inscriptions, upper left: "CP 75". Lower right: "To Mr. Tyler—remembrance of Romania—and the painter / C Petrescu 75"

In April 2007 Geoffrey wrote to Corneliu and Mariana that he had "hung the two portraits done in 1975, a very fine one of you Corneliu and a rather more rushed one done of Mariana, when I was there during the first visit after you and I met in Washington, Corneliu. That really was a wonderful time. I should not have collected my salary because it was so pleasant to be with you both that it did not really seem like work. Seeing your studio for the first time, Corneliu, and the rich treasure trove of Petrescu paintings, helping you shopping in the dollar shops, Mariana, and getting to know you both. The self-portrait, done before I arrived, was inscribed very formally to 'Mr. Tyler', whereas the one of you, Mariana, when we had all become very good friends, is inscribed to 'Geoffrey'."[18]

(Plate illustration on page 12)

23. *Mariana*
1975, oil on paper, 32.4 × 32.4 cm
(12¾ × 12¾ in.), UTT 2017/077

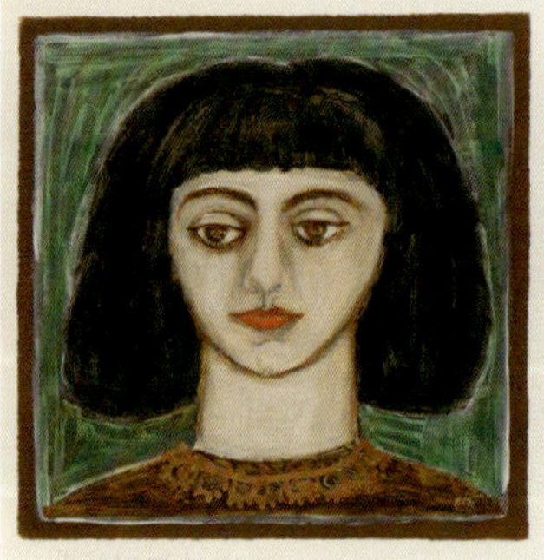

Inscriptions, lower right: "CP 75". Below: "To Geoffrey with friendship—Mariana 25 V 1975"

(Plate illustration on page 13)

24. *Icon*
1975, mixed media on artists' board,
35.2 × 28.6 cm (13⅞ × 11¼ in.), UTT 2017/046

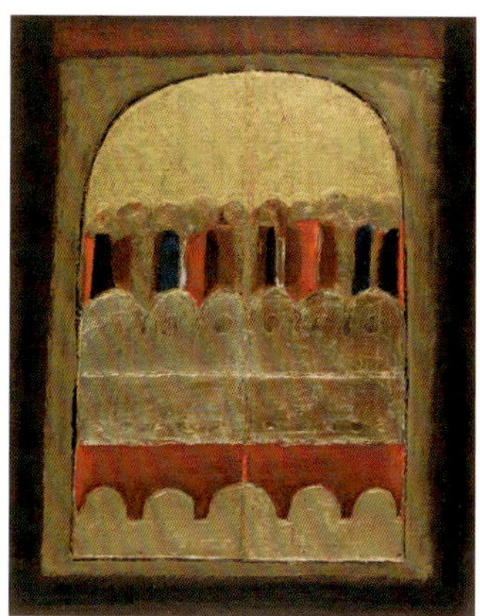

Inscription, upper left: "CP 75"

25. *Landscape*
1975, mixed media on artists' board,
30 × 40.6 cm (12 × 16⅞ in.), UTT 2017/086

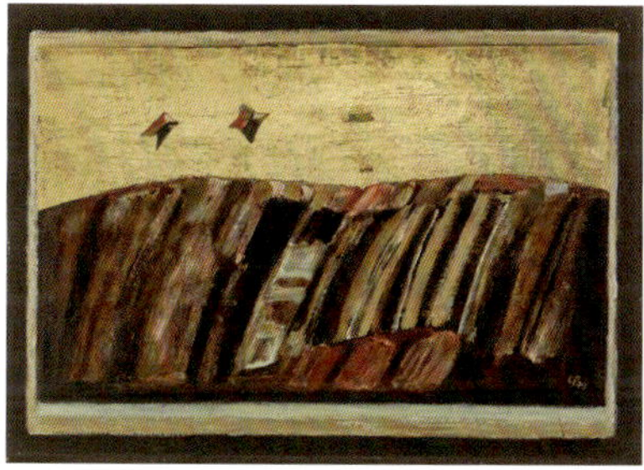

Inscription, lower right: "CP 75"

Gold leaf, a hallmark of Byzantine art, pervades Petrescu's work. It was hard to find in Romania during Ceauşescu's rule, however, and Geoffrey would bring a supply from Washington.

26. *Fluture (Butterfly)*
1975, collage and mixed media on artists' board, 38.4 × 46 cm (15⅛ × 18⅛ in.), UTT 2017/081

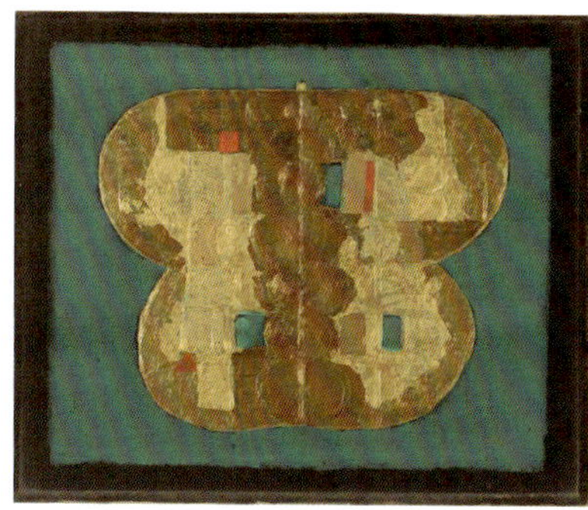

Inscriptions, lower right: "CP 75". Verso: Faint circular stamp in red ink over label: "Union of fine Arts / Calea Victorei 155 — Bucharest / ROMANIA / No. 10 / Author Corneliu Petrescu / Title of work Fluture / Media [illegible handwriting in Romanian] / Size 38 × 45 cm Price"

Geoffrey arranged for two exhibitions of Petrescu's work at the International Monetary Fund. At one of them, his wife Maria purchased this work.

(Plate illustration on page 28)

27. *Mirror*
Undated, mixed media on wood frame,
54 × 44.7 cm (21¼ × 17⅞ in.) outside frame edge, UTT 2017/079

28. *Winter*
1975, mixed media on artists' board,
34.9 × 45.4 cm (13¾ × 17⅞ in.), UTT 2017/041

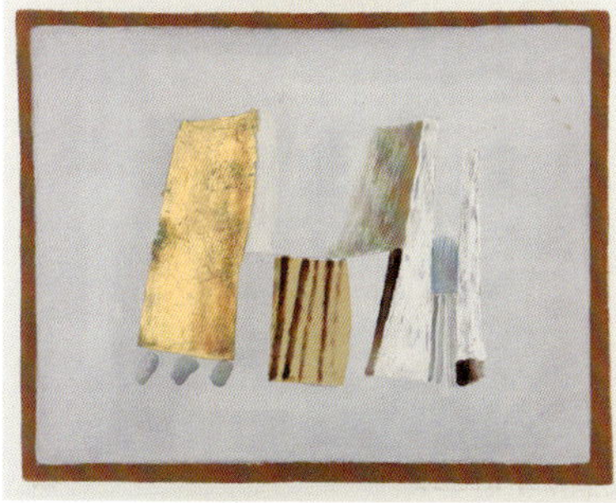

Inscriptions, lower left: "Winter". Lower right: "To Mrs and Mr Tyler — friendly — C Petrescu 75"

(Plate illustration on page 35)

29. *End of Winter*
1975, mixed media on paper, 32 × 32.4 cm (12⅝ × 12¾ in.), UTT 2017/083

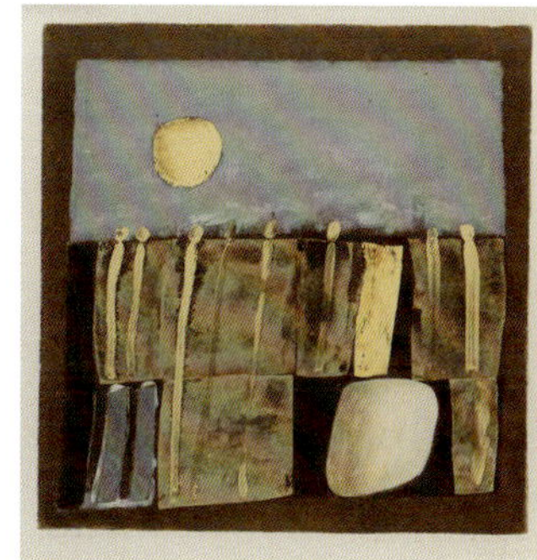

Inscriptions, lower right: "To Mrs and MR Tyler — friendly C Petrescu 75". Lower left: "End of Winter"

(Plate illustration on page 37)

30. *Untitled*
1975, mixed media on artists' board,
14.7 × 12.4 cm (5⅞ × 4⅞ in.), UTT 2017/036

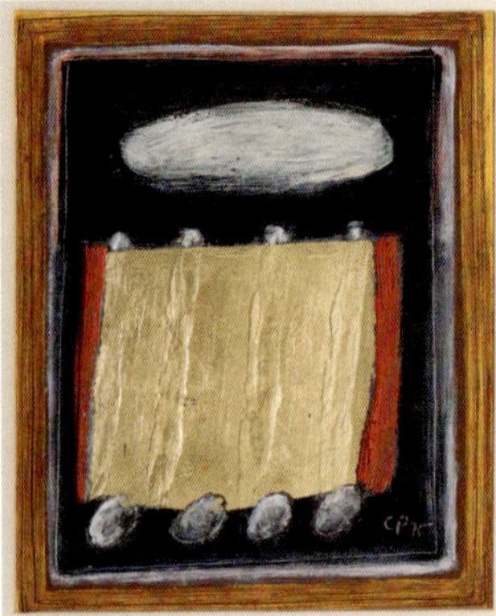

Inscription, lower right: "CP 75"

31. *Seascape*
1976, oil on paper, 32.4 × 32.4 cm
(12¾ × 12¾ in.), UTT 2017/084

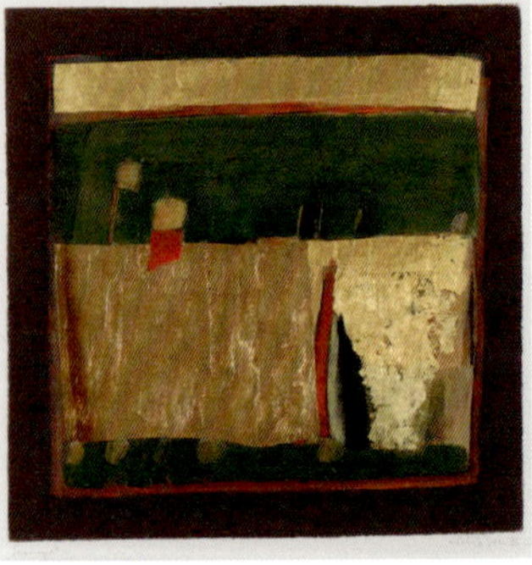

Inscription, lower right: "C Petrescu 76"

32. *Icon*
1976, mixed media on artists' board,
19 × 13.8 cm (7½ × 5½ in.), UTT 2017/038

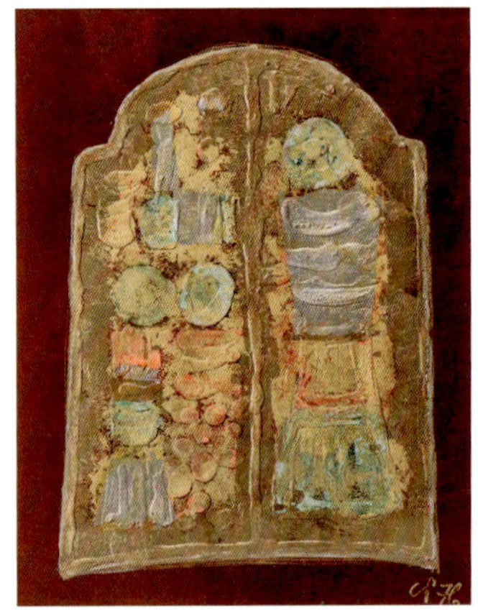

Inscriptions, lower right: "CP 76". Verso,
taped to back: "Dear Maria, Our best wishes
and warmest greetings of health and happiness for your birthday. We hope to have
the pleasure to meet you again in October.
'Happy Birthday to you!' / Corneliu and
Mariana / Bucharest — May 22"

33. *George and the Dragon*
1976, mixed media on artists' board,
30.5 × 25.4 cm (12 × 10 in.), UTT 2017/047

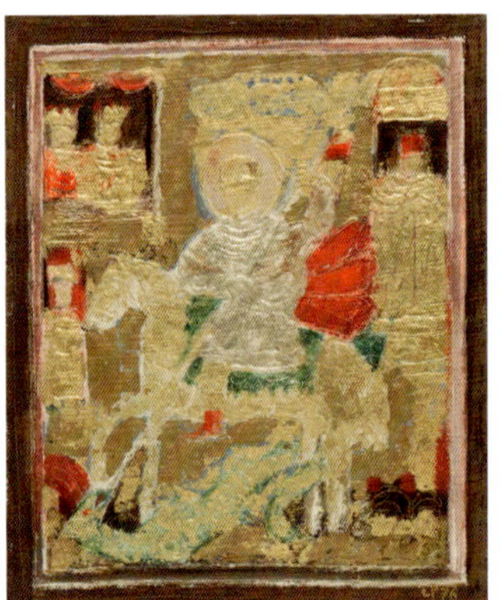

Inscriptions, lower right: "CP 76". Verso:
"To Geoffrey Tyler — my great friend — for
his birthday — . . . our life is a permanent
struggle — and there are lots of dragons. . . . /
Bucharest — June 1976 — C Petrescu"

34. *Portrait of Geoffrey Tyler*
1977, mixed media on artists' board,
43.5 × 34.9 cm (17⅛ × 12⅝ in.), UTT 2017/055

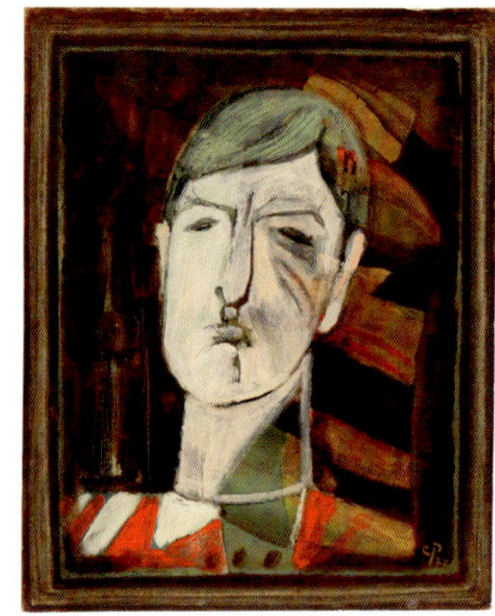

Inscription, lower right: "CP 77"

(Plate illustration on page 23)

35. *Untitled*
1977, mixed media on artists' board,
34.3 × 50.5 cm (13½ × 19⅞ in.), UTT 2017/049

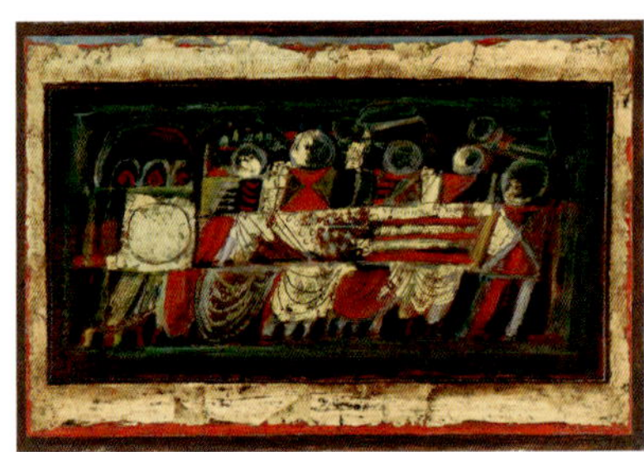

Inscription, lower left: "CP 77"

(Plate illustration on page 27)

36. *Christ in the Tomb*
1978, mixed media on artists' board,
22.9 × 30.5 cm (9 × 12 in.), UTT 2017/037

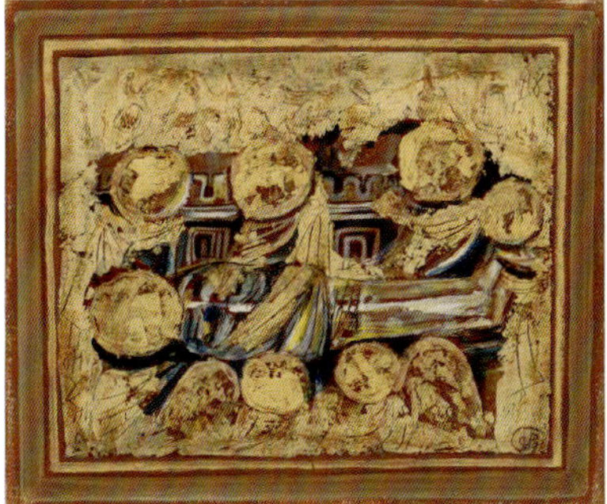

Inscription, lower right: "CP 78"

37. *Untitled*
1978, collage and mixed media on artists'
board, 34.9 × 43.8 cm (13¾ × 17¼ in.),
UTT 2017/008

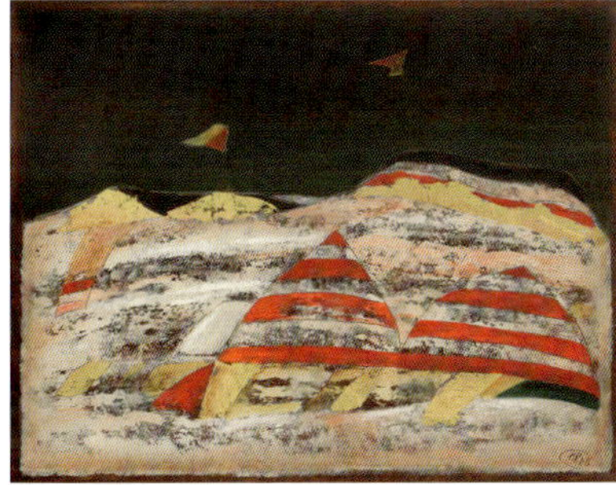

Inscription, lower right: "CP 78"

38. *Landscape*
Undated, oil on canvas, 64.8 × 80 cm
(25½ × 31½ in.), UTT 2017/085

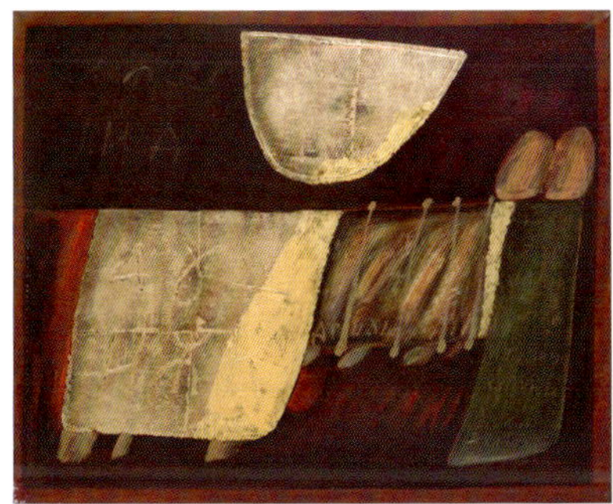

Geoffrey tried to interest Petrescu in producing larger works — they would make
the artist more money — and Petrescu did
paint this and the next one (untitled)
for Geoffrey, but the idea never took hold.

39. *Untitled*
1978, mixed media on canvas, 70.5 × 85.7 cm
(27¾ × 33¾ in.), UTT 2017/061

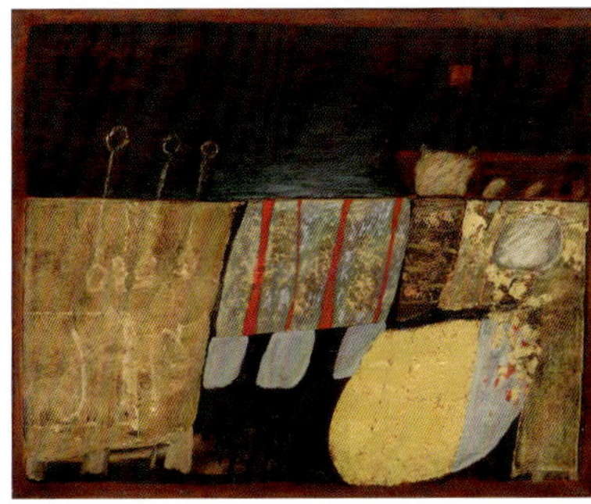

Inscription, lower right: "CP 78"

(Plate illustration on page 31)

40. *Angel*
1979, mixed media on artists' board,
14 × 10.5 cm (5½ × 4⅛ in.), UTT 2017/052

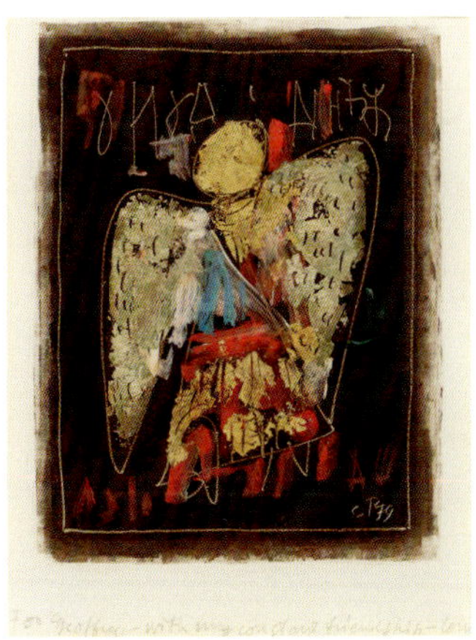

Inscriptions, lower right: "CP 79". Below:
"For Geoffrey — with my consistent friendship — Corneliu"

(Plate illustration on page 32)

41. *Icon*
1979, mixed media on artists' board,
16.2 × 13.1 cm (6⅜ × 5¼ in.), UTT 2017/039

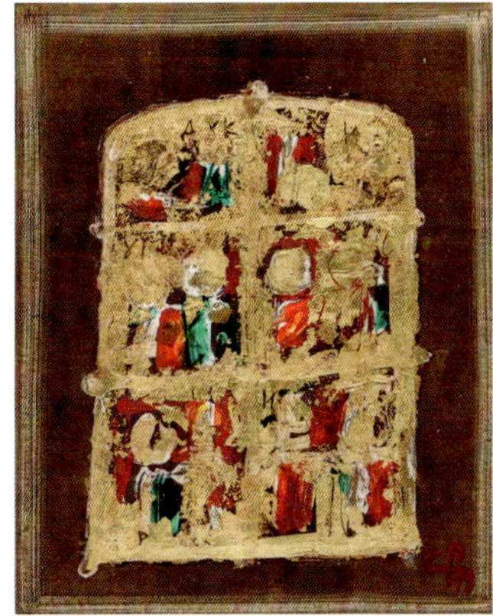

Inscription, lower right: "CP 79"

Church doors, in particular, came to interest
Petrescu. In the Orthodox Church, these
were commonly of wood with icons painted
on them. The scenes and figures in this
painting are highly abstract, "showing
nothing more than the feeling of icons."[19]

42. *Untitled*
1979, mixed media on canvas, 32.1 × 40.3 cm
(12⅝ × 15⅞ in.), UTT 2017/060

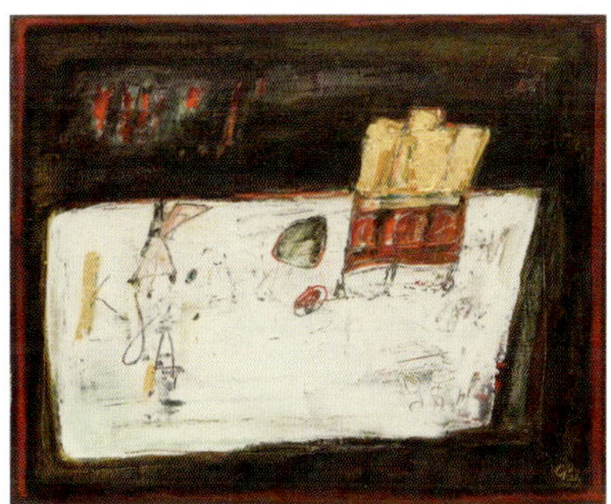

Inscription, lower right: "CP 79"

(Plate illustration on page 30)

43. *Christmas Card*
1979, collage and mixed media on
cardboard, 10.2 × 8.9 cm (4 × 3½ in.),
UTT 2017/080

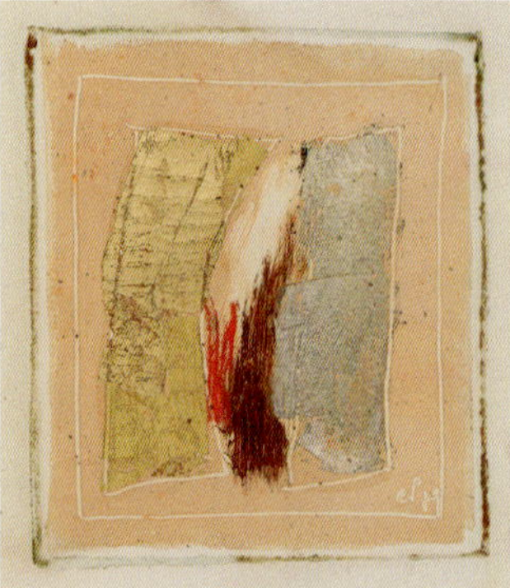

Inscriptions, lower right: "CP 79". Verso:
"For both of you — from me and Mariana —
for Christmas and the New Year — our best
wishes of health and happiness. We are
hoping to meet you — very soon — here —
or there.... / Corneliu Mariana Buc. Nov. 79"

This card was sent to me and my then
husband.

44. *Icon*
1980, collage and mixed media on
artists' board, 40.6 × 33 cm (16 × 13 in.),
UTT 2017/062

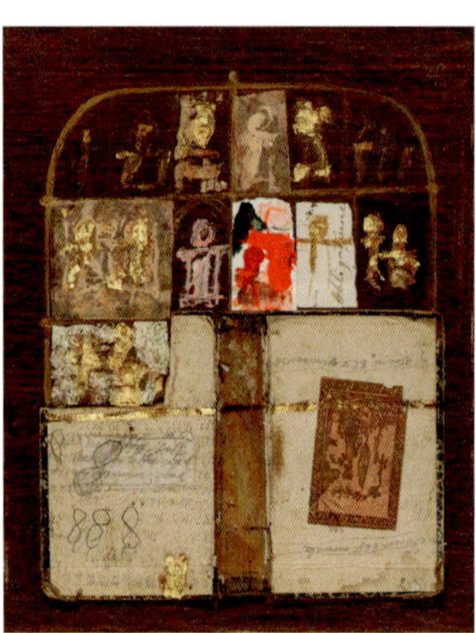

Inscription, upper right: "CP 80"

The "overall door design remains" in this
work, "but the collage and painting are sec-
ular rather than religious," continuing the
trend that Geoffrey has noted. This work
"has as its base a found object, the cover of
an old schoolbook, glued to the canvas.
The child's scribblings on the inside of the
cover of the book — it is the inside that is
seen — upside down to add to the abstrac-
tion, are untouched by Petrescu."[20]

45. *Icon*
1980 or 1986, collage and mixed media on
artists' board, 40.6 × 33.3 cm (16 × 13⅛ in.),
UTT 2017/063

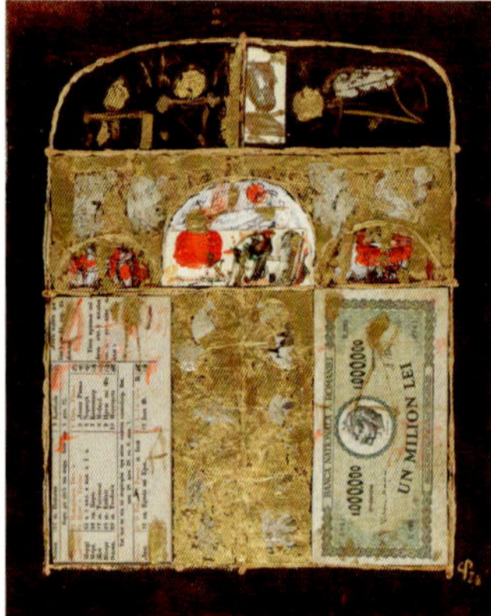

Inscription, lower right: "CP 80/86"?

In the Ceaușescu years, the value of the
Romanian currency had deteriorated and
food was being rationed, underpinning
the growing political crisis.

The date of this painting, in a roughly
brushed inscription, is hard to read.

(Plate illustration on page 33)

46. *Untitled*
1980, collage and mixed media on artists'
board, 46 × 36.8 cm (18⅛ × 14½ in.),
UTT 2017/078

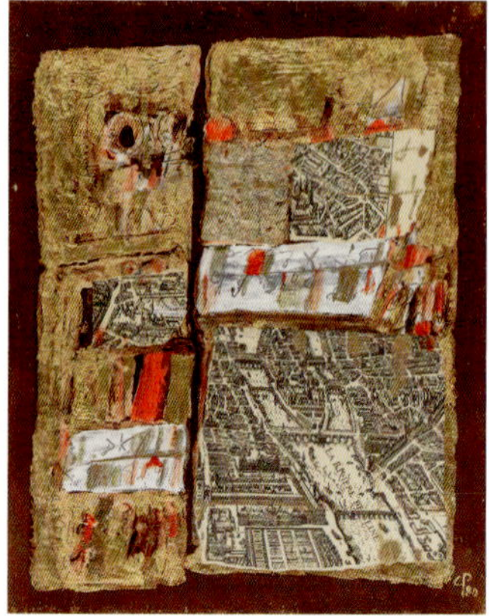

Inscription, lower right: "CP 80"

The collaged elements are "sections of a 17th
century map of Paris streets and buildings."[22]
A major source of materials for Petrescu's
collages was bookstalls on the left embank-
ment of the Seine, although the main source
was in Romania: old letters, stamps, and
religious documents in Old Church Slavonic.

(Plate illustration on page 42)

47. *Flowers*
1981, mixed media on artists' board,
40.6 × 33 cm (16 × 13 in.), UTT 2017/087

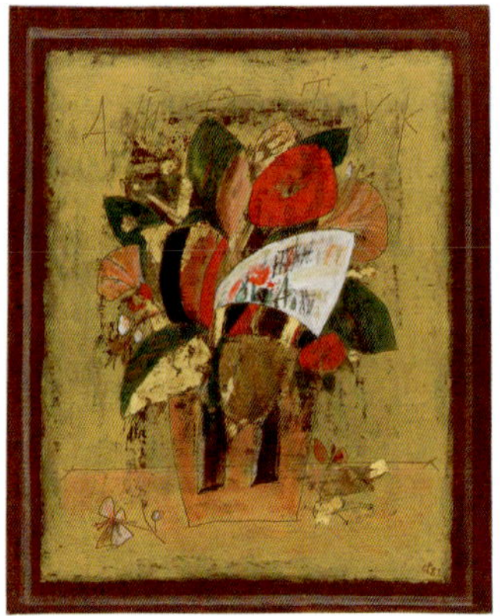

Inscription, lower right: "CP 81"

(Plate illustration on page 29)

48. *Dusty Memories*
1982, collage and mixed media on artists' board, 30.8 × 40.3 cm (12⅛ × 15⅞ in.), UTT 2017/050

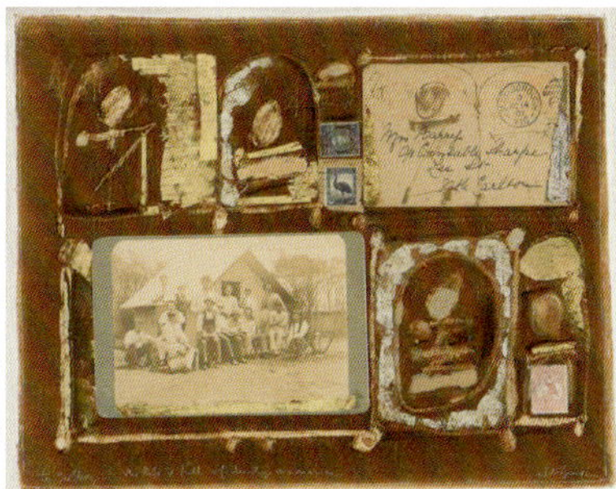

Inscriptions, lower right: "C Petrescu". Lower left: "To Geoffrey, the life is full of dusty memories…."

The collaged elements were supplied by Geoffrey. They incorporate a photograph of his "grandfather taken in the 19th century at a gold mining camp in the desert, with a group of prospectors. Another part of the painting contains the cover of a letter written by the grandfather and some old Australian stamps."[21]

(Plate illustration on page 39)

49. *Untitled*
1986, collage and mixed media on artists' board, 31.1 × 39.1 cm (12¼ × 15⅜ in.), UTT 2017/048

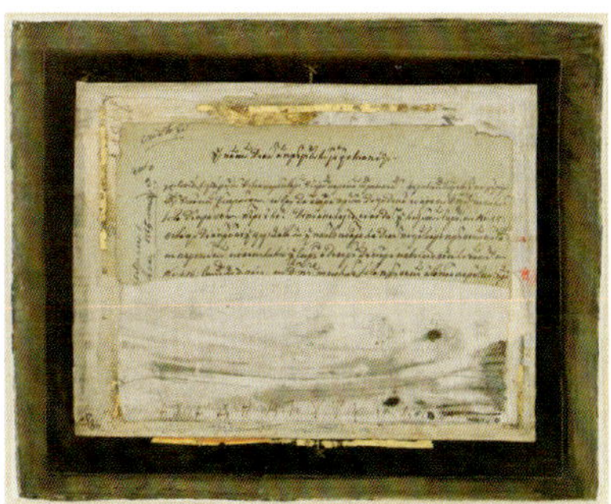

Inscription, lower left: "CP 86"

50. *Landscape*
1987, collage and mixed media on artists' board, 16.5 × 22.2 cm (6½ × 8¾ in.), UTT 2017/003

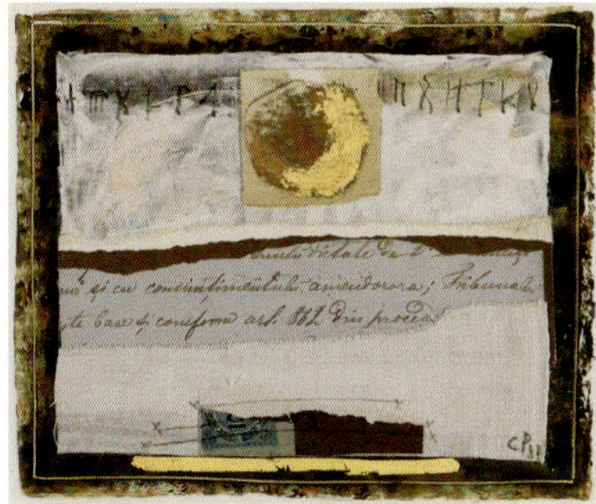

Inscription, lower right: "CP 87"

Geoffrey gave this as a gift to me.

(Plate illustration on page 38)

51. *Sandcastle*
1995, mixed media on artists' board, 31.4 × 39.4 cm (12⅜ × 15½ in., UTT 2017/004

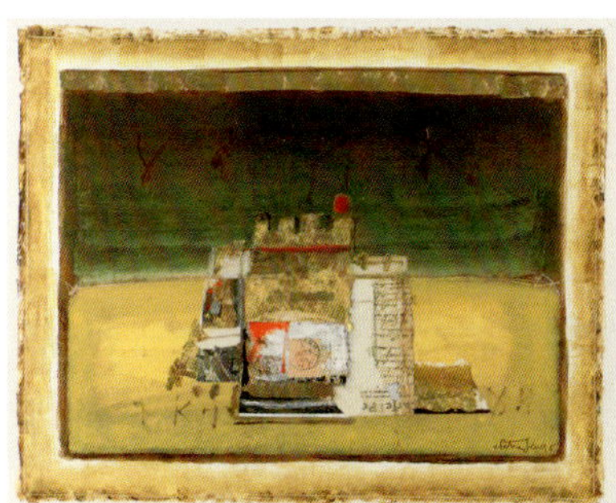

Inscription, lower right: "C Petrescu 95"

(Plate illustration on page 41)

52. *Untitled*
1995, collage and mixed media on artists' board, 30.5 × 38.7 cm (12 × 15¼ in.), UTT 2017/007

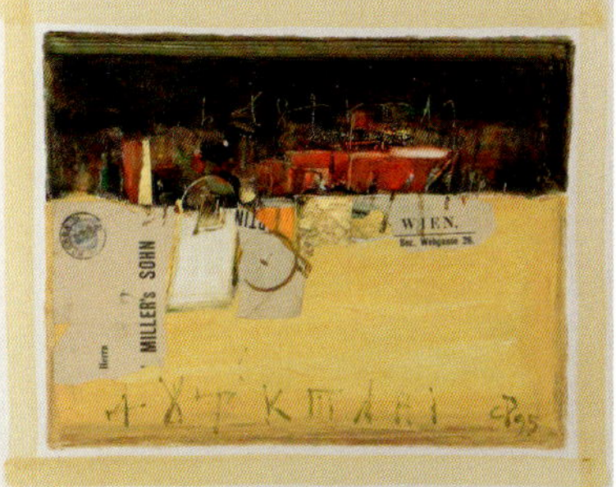

Inscription, lower right: "CP 95"

The lettering—seen in the foreground here and in many Petrescu works—is derived from Slavonic script, but has no literal meaning and is purely decorative.

53. *Desert*
1995, collage and mixed media on artists' board, 31.1 × 24.8 cm (12¼ × 9¾ in.), UTT 2017/073

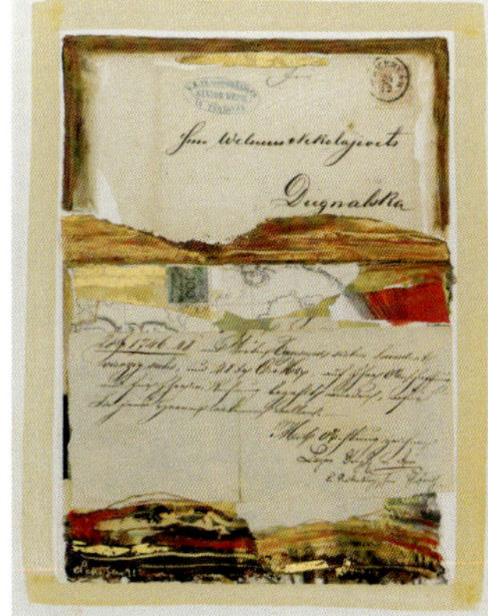

Inscriptions, lower right: "C Petrescu 95". Verso label: "Corneliu Petrescu 'Desert'—32 × 25 mixed media collage"

(Plate illustration on page 40)

54. *Autumn*
1996, collage and mixed media on artists'
board, 31.1 × 24.4 cm (12¼ × 9⅝ in.),
UTT 2017/072

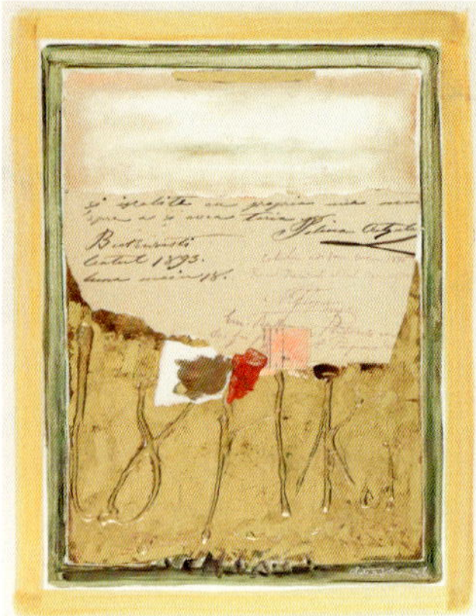

Inscription, verso: "Corneliu Petrescu
'Autumn' 32 × 35 — 1996 mixed media and
collage, Toamni C Petrescu 96"

55. *Untitled*
1996, collage and mixed media on artists'
board, 24.8 × 31.1 cm (9¾ × 12¼ in.),
UTT 2017/006

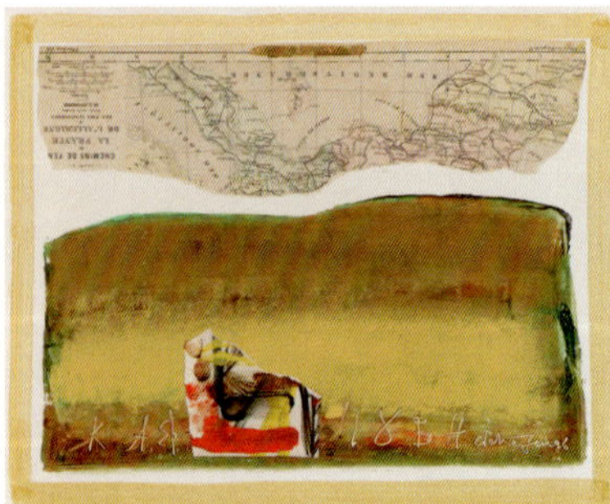

Inscription, lower right: "C Petrescu 96"

56. *Winter*
1997, collage and mixed media on artists'
board, 24.8 × 31.4 cm (9¾ × 12⅜ in.),
UTT 2017/043

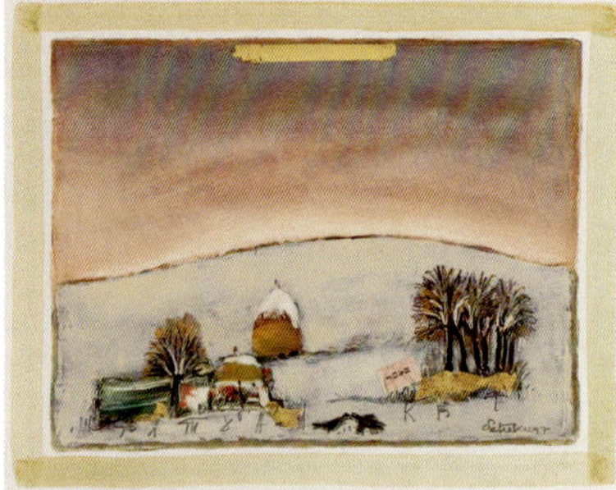

Inscription, lower right: "C Petrescu 97"

57. *Winter*
1997, collage and mixed media on artists'
board, 30.5 × 38.8 cm (12 × 15¼ in.),
UTT 2017/042

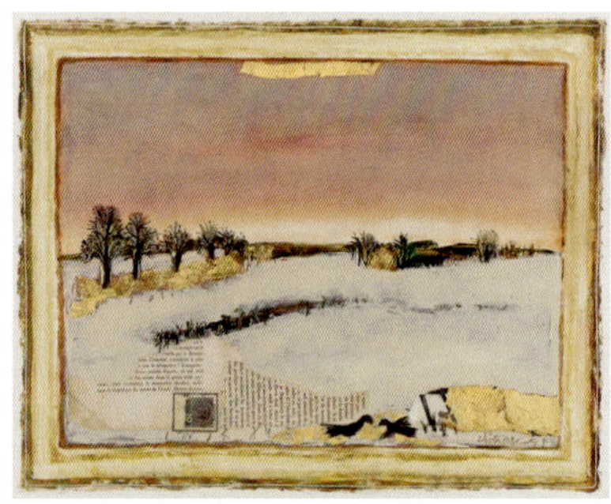

Inscription, lower right: "C Petrescu 97"

(Plate illustration on page 34)

58. *Shore*
1998, mixed media on artists' board,
30.2 × 38.7 cm (11⅞ × 15¼ in.), UTT 2017/005

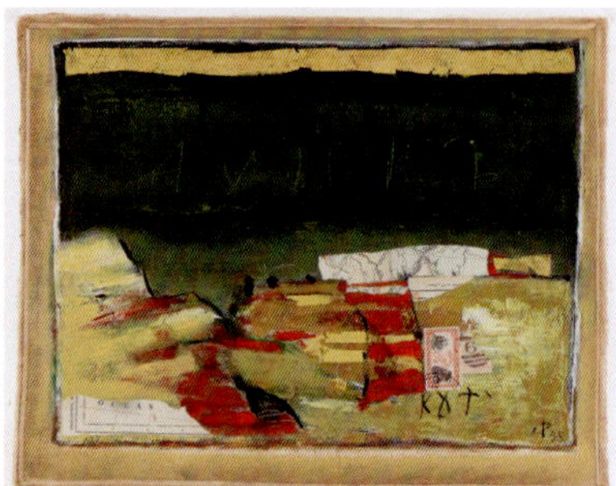

Inscription, lower right: "CP 98"

59. *Desert*
1999, collage and mixed media on artists'
board, 33.7 × 27 cm (13¼ × 10⅝ in.),
UTT 2017/074

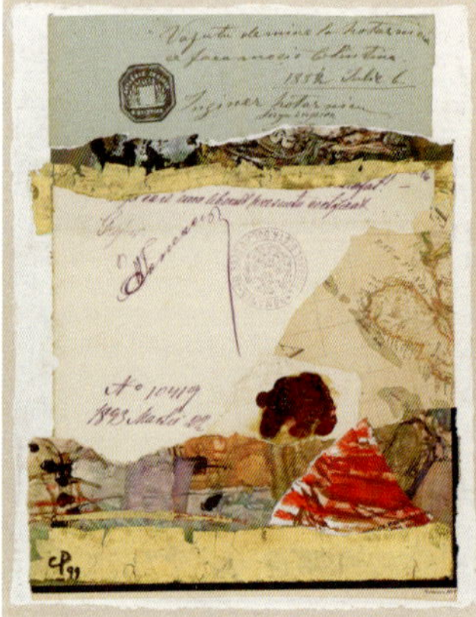

Inscriptions, lower right: "CP 99".
Verso label: "Corneliu Petrescu 'Desert' —
32 × 25 mixed media collage"

60. *Untitled*
1999, collage and mixed media on artists' board, 30.5 × 38.4 cm (12 × 15⅛ in.), UTT 2017/088

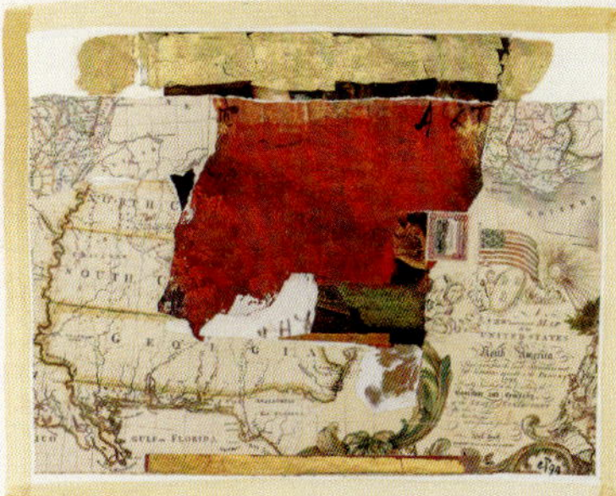

Inscription, lower right: "CP 99"

The large collage piece here is a map of part of the United States — a fine engraved one, dated 1786.

The Petrescus made several visits to the United States, largely organized by Geoffrey, who accompanied them. They travelled around the West Coast on one visit, and around Florida on another, and the scenery profoundly influenced Corneliu's work.

(Plate illustration on page 43)

61. *Winter*
2000, collage and mixed media on artists' board, 25.1 × 31.8 cm (9⅞ × 12½ in.), UTT 2017/044

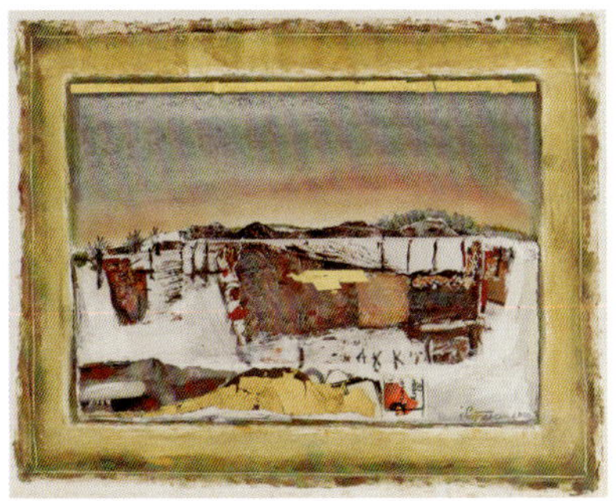

Inscription, lower right: "C Petrescu 2000"

Silvia Radu, born 1935

62. *Small Bowl with Lip*
1981, glazed porcelain, 3 × 9.5 cm (1⅛ × 3¾ in.) variable, UTT 2017/016

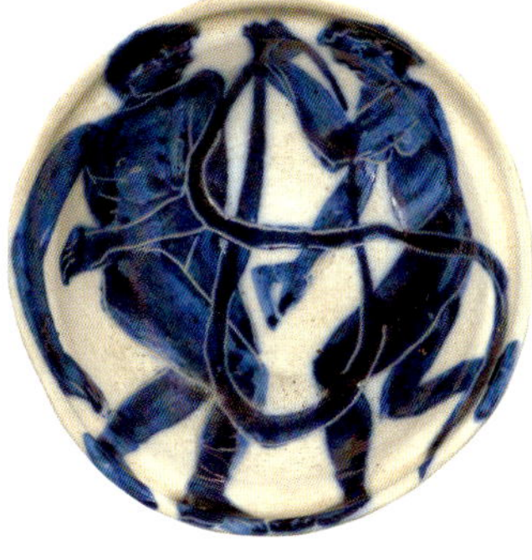

Inscription on bottom: "SR 81"

Geoffrey's collection includes a vast number of Silvia's ceramics, particularly these small bowls, which she turned out and sold in great quantity. She and her husband had introduced Geoffrey to many artists — Georgeta Năpăruș, Octav Grigorescu, Horia Bernea, Ovidiu Maitec, Geta Bratescu, Ștefan Câlția, and others. On my more recent visits to her, she carried on with this, introducing me to many interesting friends of hers. Rachael Rose, Curator of the Tyler Collection from UTAS, and I were there to celebrate her birthday in 2018.

63. *Small Bowl with Lip*
1982, glazed porcelain, 3.5 × 10 cm (1⅜ × 3⅞ in.), UTT 2017/017

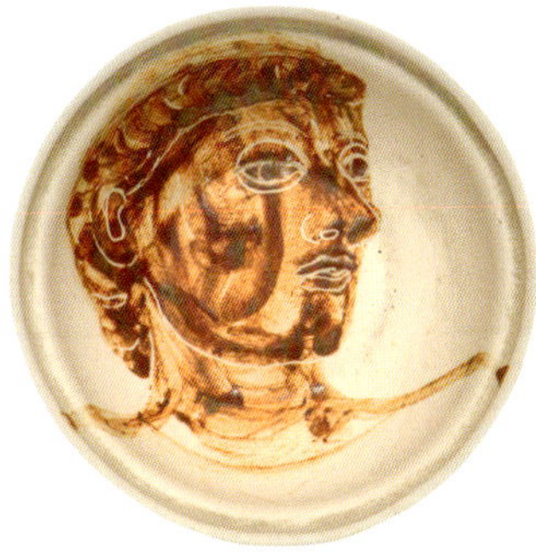

Inscription on bottom: "SR 82"

64. *Small Bowl with Lip*
1987, glazed porcelain, 3.5 × 9.5 cm (1⅜ × 3¾ in.) variable, UTT 2017/034

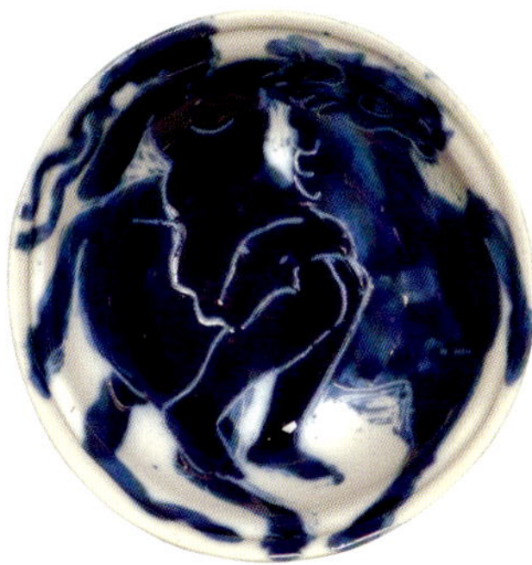

Inscription on side: "Silvia Radu 87"

65. *Small Bowl*
Undated, glazed porcelain, 4.7 × 11.4 cm (1⅞ × 4⅜ in.) variable, UTT 2017/024

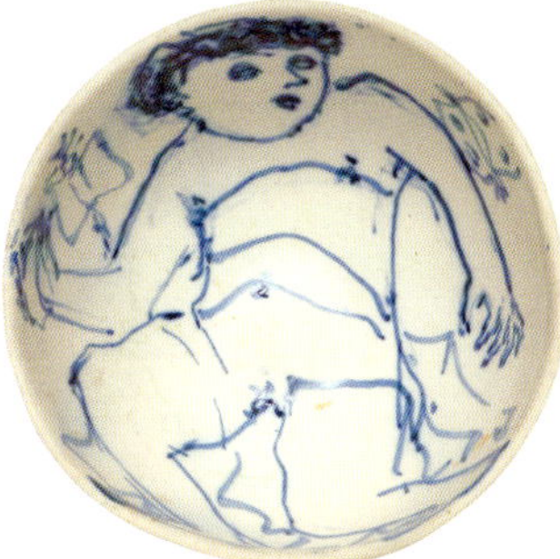

Inscription on side: "SR" and flower designs

Silvia gave this to me in the late 1970s or 1980s.

(Plate illustration on page 60)

66. *Small Bowl*
1982, glazed porcelain, 5 × 11.3 cm
(2 × 4.5 in.) variable, UTT 2017/023

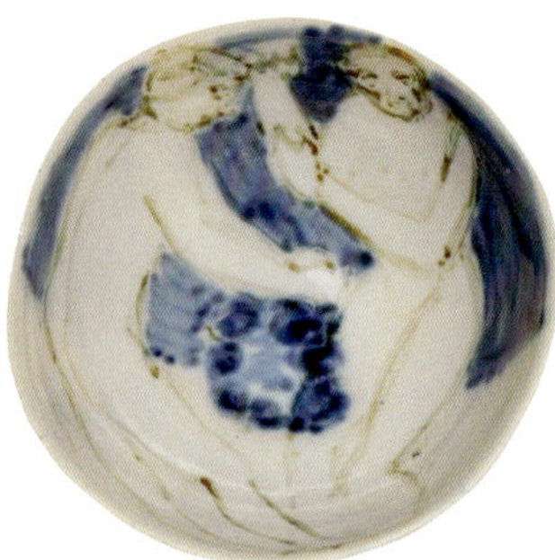

Inscription on side: "SR 82" and stripe designs

67. *Small Bowl*
Undated, glazed porcelain, 4.4 × 11.2 cm
(1¾ × 4⅜ in.) variable, UTT 2017/025

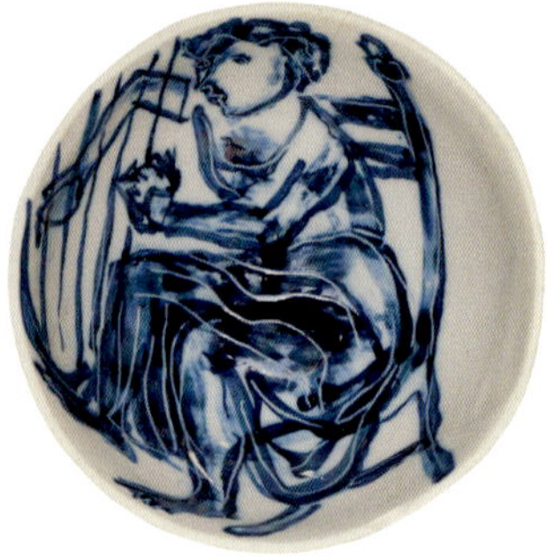

Inscription on side: "SR" and flower designs

68. *Small Bowl*
Undated, glazed porcelain, 4.4 × 10.8 cm
(1¾ × 4¼ in.) variable, UTT 2017/022

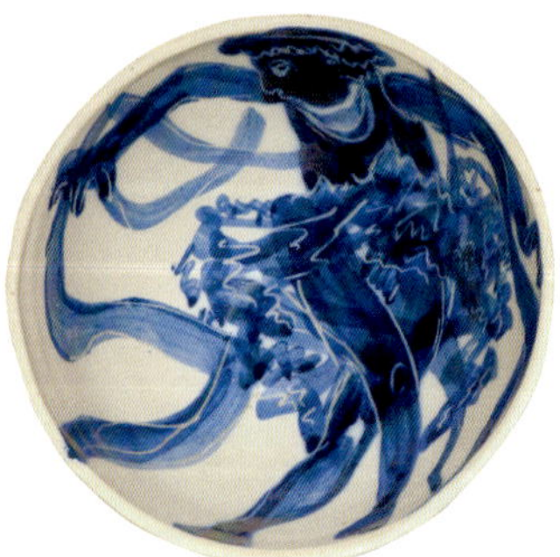

69. *Flat Bowl*
Undated, glazed porcelain, 3.3 × 13.5 cm
(1⅓ × 5⅜ in.) variable, UTT 2017/019

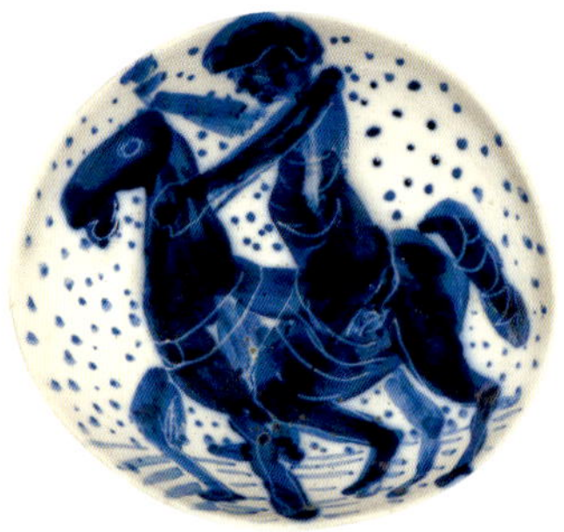

Inscription on bottom: "SR"

(Plate illustration on page 61, top)

70. *Flat Bowl*
Undated, glazed porcelain, 3.2 × 13.5 cm
(1¼ × 5⅓ in.) variable, UTT 2017/018

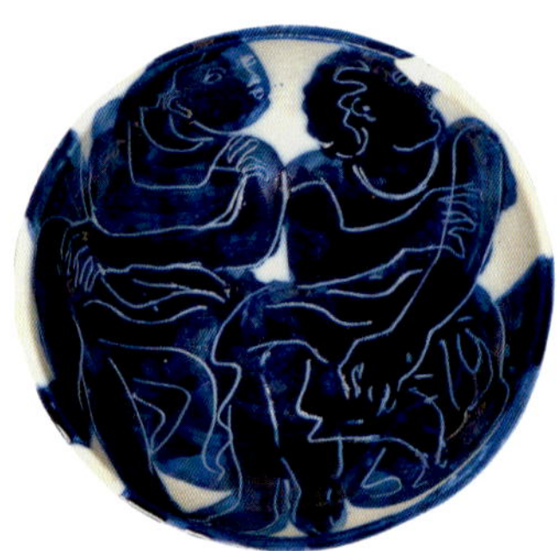

Inscription on bottom: "SR" and pattern along side edge

71. *Flat Bowl*
1986, glazed porcelain, 3 × 13.3 cm
(1¼ × 5⅓ in.) variable, UTT 2017/020

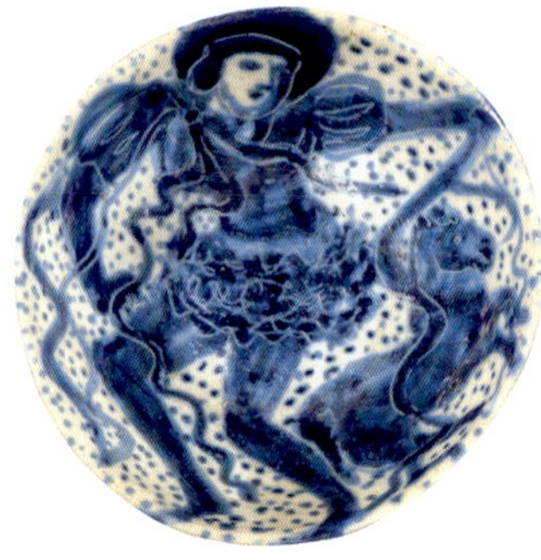

Inscription on side: "Silvia Radu 86"

This bowl was on display at the symposium "Cultural Identity, Geography of Encounter, & the Politics of Space/Time," along with works by Petrescu brought by Curator and Registrar Rachael Rose from the University of Tasmania. The symposium was at Columbia University in New York in April 2019. Organized by Professor Mona Momescu, the speakers were Rose, Jeff Malpas, and Éduard Andrei.

72. *Flat Bowl*
Undated, glazed porcelain, 3 × 13.5 cm
(1¼ × 5⅓ in.) variable, UTT 2017/031

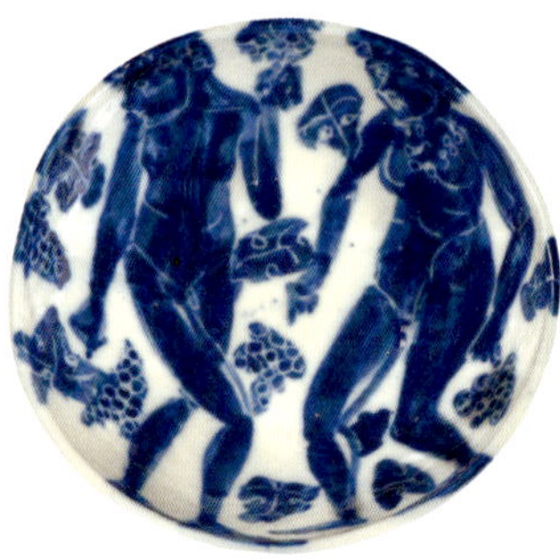

Inscriptions on side: "SR" and flower designs

(Plate illustration on page 61, bottom)

73. *Medium Bowl*
1982, glazed porcelain, 5.7 × 16.5 cm
(2¼ × 6½ in.), UTT 2017/026

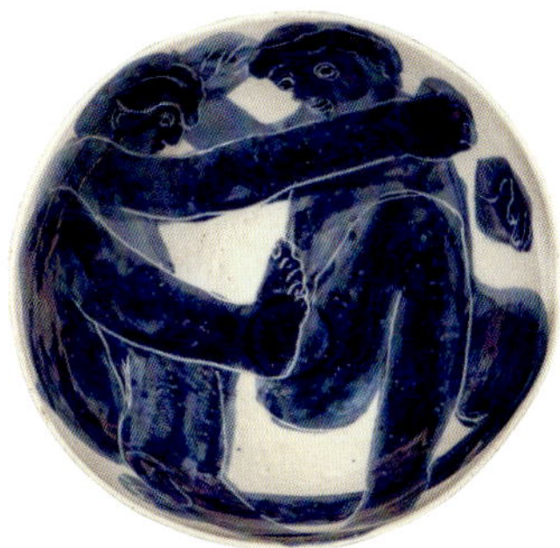

Inscription on side: "SR 82" and design
of bow and ribbon

74. *Bowl with Stand*
Undated, glazed porcelain, 9.5 × 16.3 cm
(4 × 6½ in.) variable, UTT 2017/028

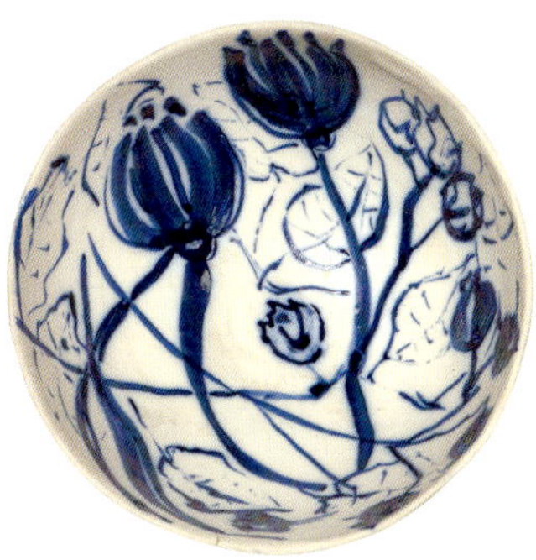

Inscription on side: "SR" and flower designs
and patterns

(Plate illustration on page 62)

75. *Bowl with Stand*
2009, glazed porcelain, 9.1 × 16.5 cm
(3½ × 6½ in.) variable, UTT 2017/035

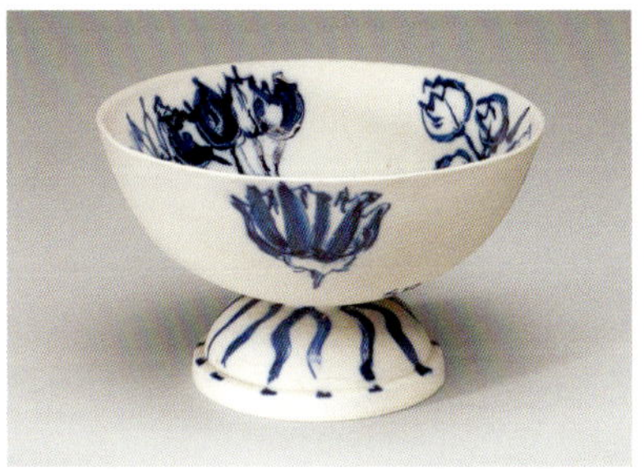

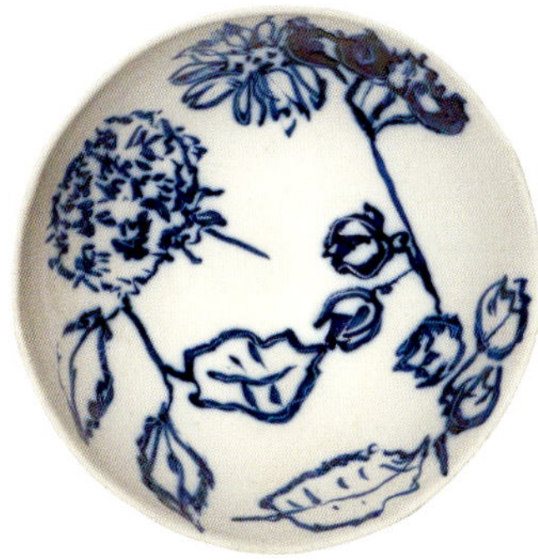

Inscription on side: "SR" and flower designs
and stripes

76. *Large Bowl*
Undated, glazed porcelain, 5.8 × 24.2 cm
(2¼ × 9½ in.), UTT 2017/027

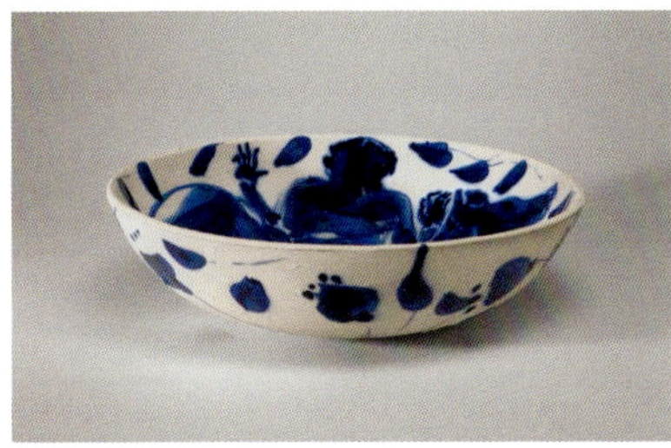

Inscription on side: "SR" and leaf and flower
designs

(Plate illustration on page 63)

77. *Large Bowl*
1987, glazed porcelain, 7.1 × 25.5 cm
(2¾ × 10 in.), UTT 2017/030

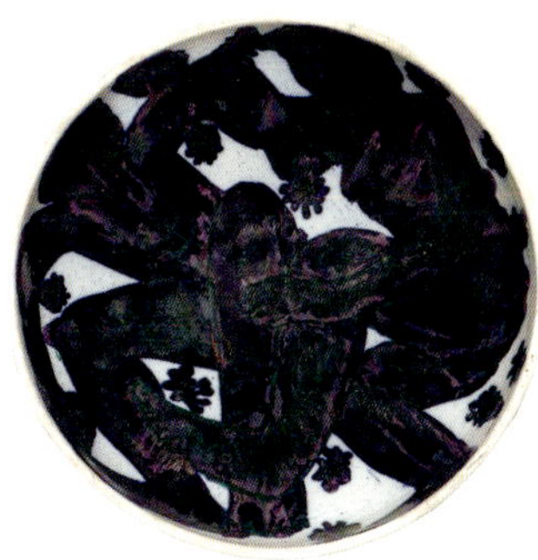

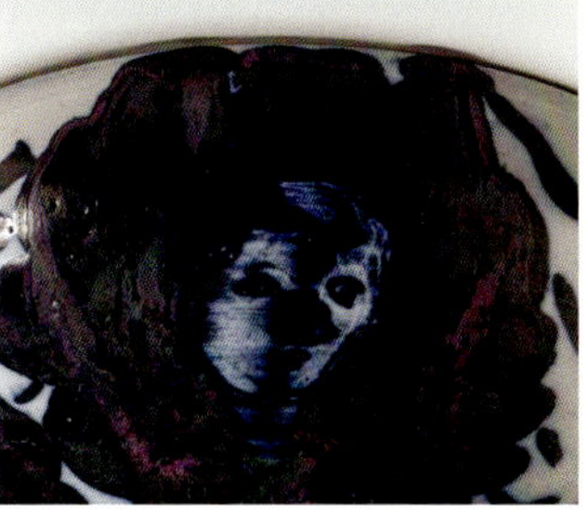

Inscription on side: "Silvia Radu 87" and
patterns with faces

78. *Vase*
Undated, glazed porcelain, 24 × 7.7 cm
(9 × 3¹⁄₁₆ in.) variable, UTT 2017/029

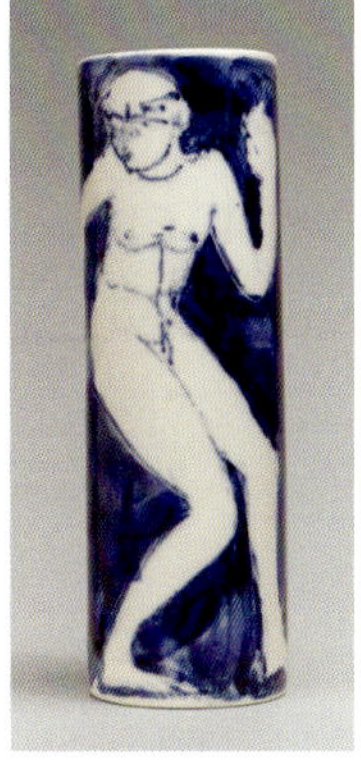
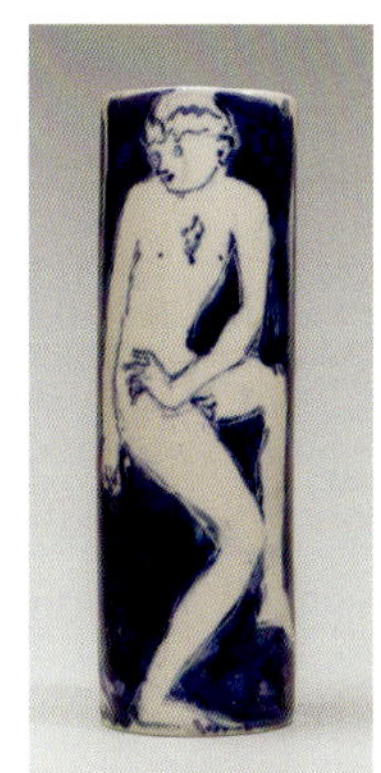

79. *Vase*
Undated, glazed porcelain, 22.7 × 7.3 cm
(8⅞ × 3¹⁄₁₆ in.) variable, UTT 2017/101

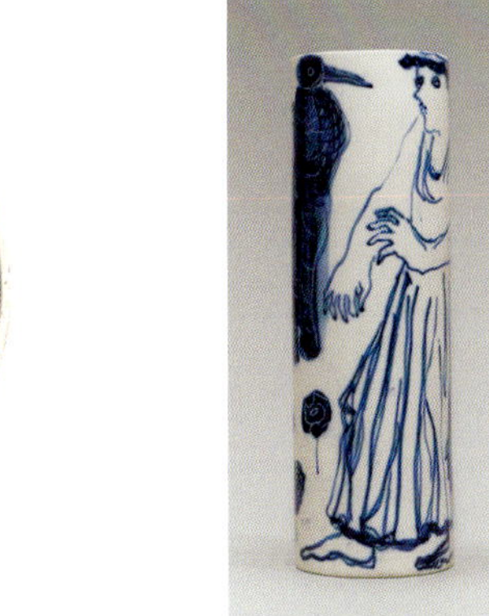
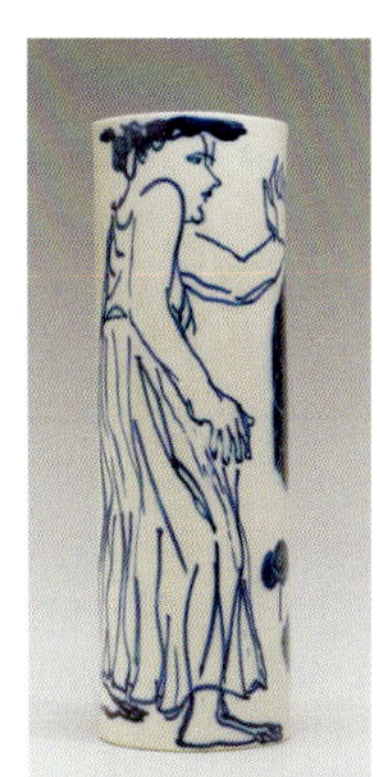

80. *Large Vase*
Undated, glazed porcelain, 32.7 × 11.8 cm
(12⅞ × 4⅔ in.), UTT 2017/032

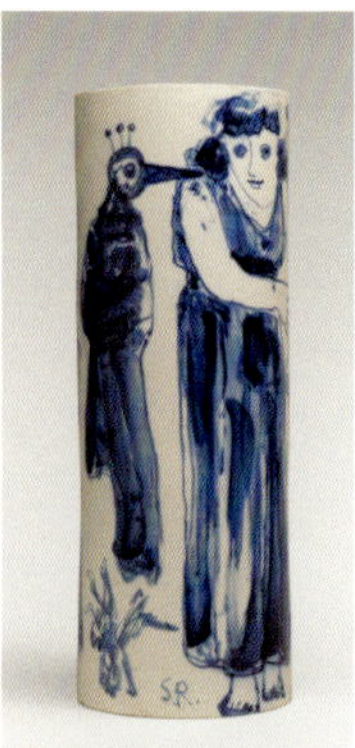 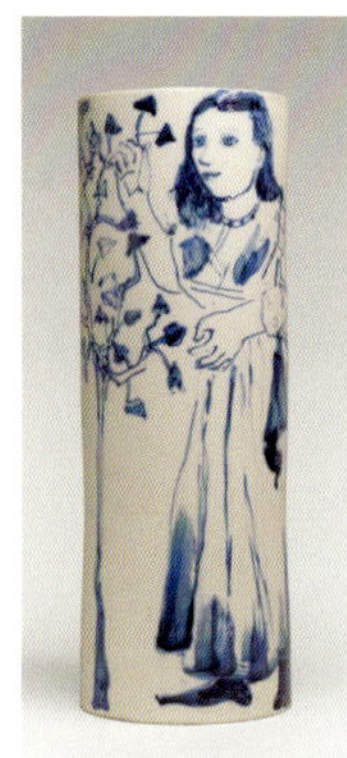

Inscription: "SR"

(Plate illustration on page 64)

81. *Large Vase*
Undated, glazed porcelain, 33.2 × 11.7 cm
(13 × 4⅔ in.), UTT 2017/033

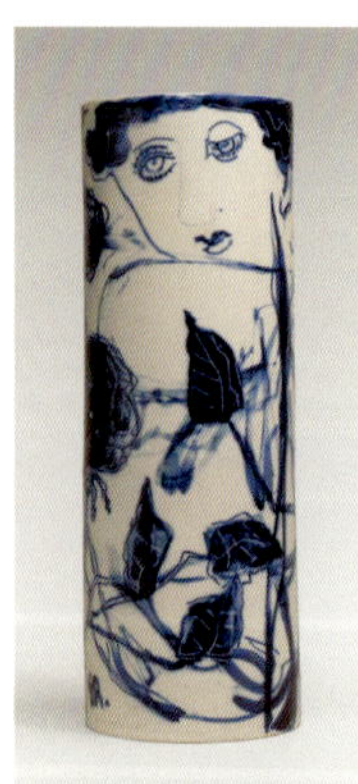 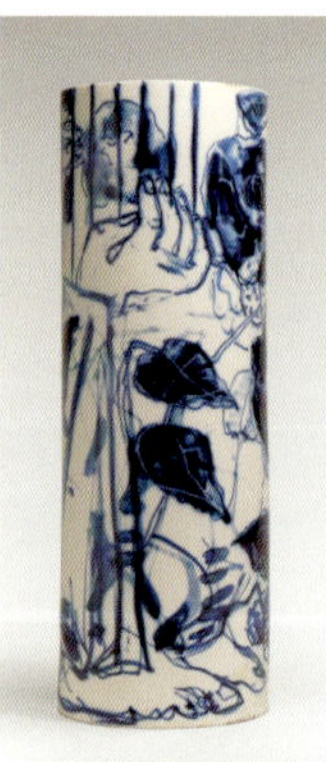

Inscription: "SR"

(Plate illustration on page 65)

82. *Plaque*
Undated, glazed porcelain,
13.4 × 12.4 × 0.6 cm (5⅜ × 4⅞ ×¼ in.)
variable, UTT 2017/021

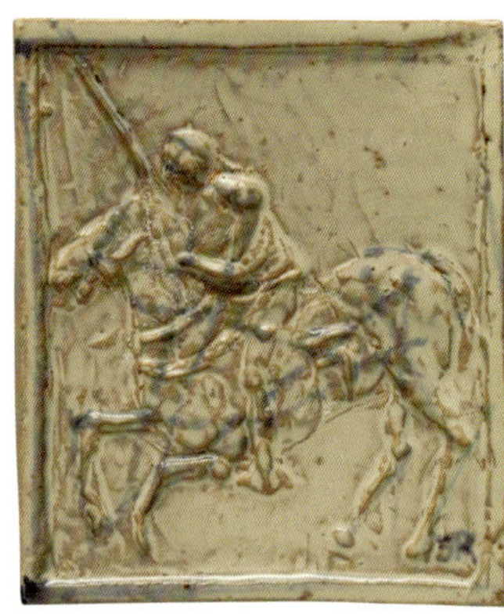

Inscription at lower right: "SR"

83. *Bookend*
Undated, glazed porcelain, 11.6 × 13.5 × 9 cm
(4½ × 5⅓ × 3½ in.) variable, UTT 2017/012

84. *Bookend*
Undated, glazed porcelain, 11.6 × 11.5 × 8.8 cm
(4½ × 4½ × 3½ in.) variable, UTT 2017/013

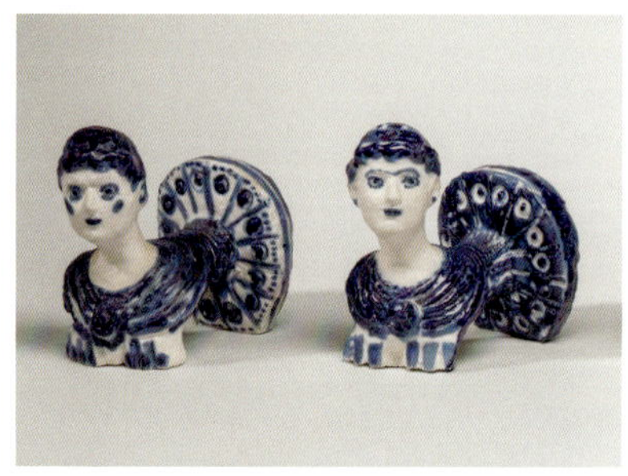

(Plate illustrations on page 66)

85. *Bookend*
Undated, glazed porcelain, 12 × 11.3 × 9.7 cm
(4¾ × 4½ × 3¾ in.) variable, UTT 2017/014

86. *Bookend*
Undated, glazed porcelain, 11.1 × 11.7 × 8.8 cm
(4⅓ × 4⅔ × 3½ in.) variable, UTT 2017/015

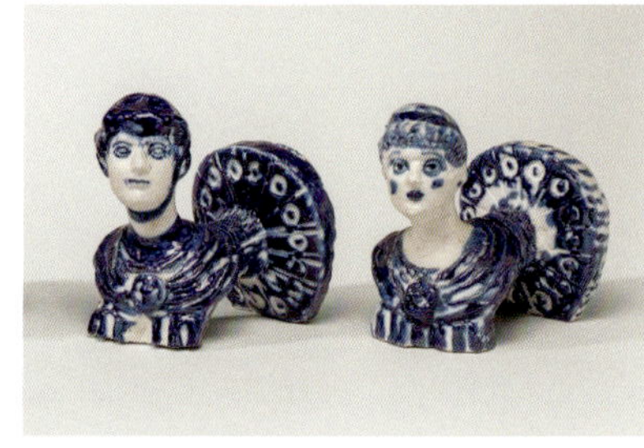

(Plate illustrations on page 66)

87. *Man and Woman*
Undated, 13.3 × 5.4 × 4.4 cm
(5¼ × 2⅛ × 1¾ in.) variable, UTT 2021/001

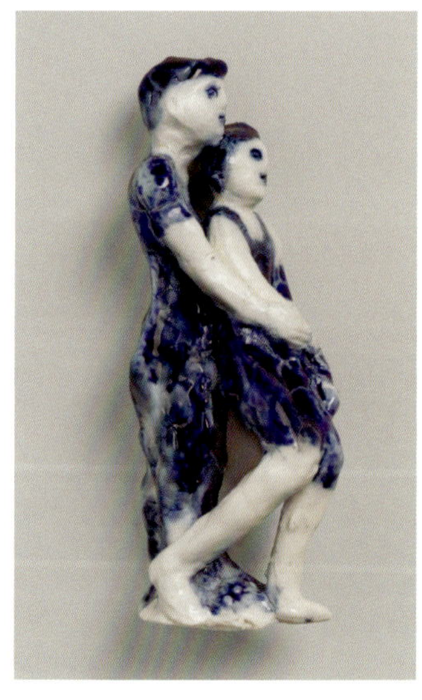

88. *Nude with Robe*
1983, glazed porcelain, 34 × 20 × 9 cm
(13⅜ × 7⅞ × 3½ in.) variable, UTT 2017/093

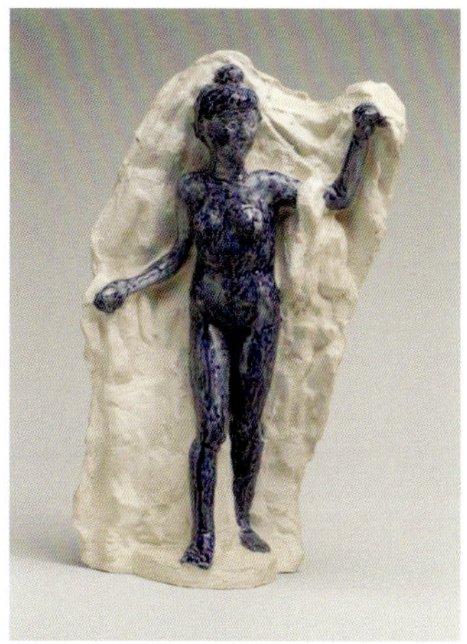

Inscription on verso, lower left: "SR 83"

(Plate illustration on page 67)

Gheorghe Şaru, 1920–2003

89. *Untitled*
1968, oil on canvas, 81 × 110 cm
(31⅞ × 43¼ in.), UTT 2017/069

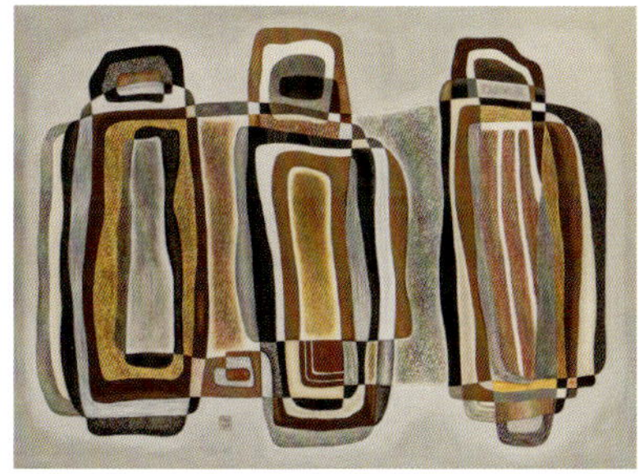

Inscription, lower left: "Saru 1968"

"Yesterday I spent a little time adjusting a painting above the fireplace in the living room. It is one by Saru and a good example of his work at the time. It is big, about 1.20 m long and 0.75 m. in height, a big work. Previously there had been a somewhat smaller painting there and . . . I used the same hook . . . on which to hang it. . . . this left the Saru a little too low but it was difficult to make it higher because the Saru is big and heavy and really needs two people to hang it. However, I managed to work out a method. . . . It is amazing how such a simple thing as the height of a painting can affect its appearance."[23] The painting hangs over my own fireplace to this day. It has just undergone conservation.

Şaru lived the final twenty years of his life in the United States.

(Plate illustration on page 69)

90. *Forme in Spaţiu (Shapes in Space)*
1976, oil on canvas, 49.5 × 64.5 cm
(19½ × 25⅜ in.), UTT 2017/068

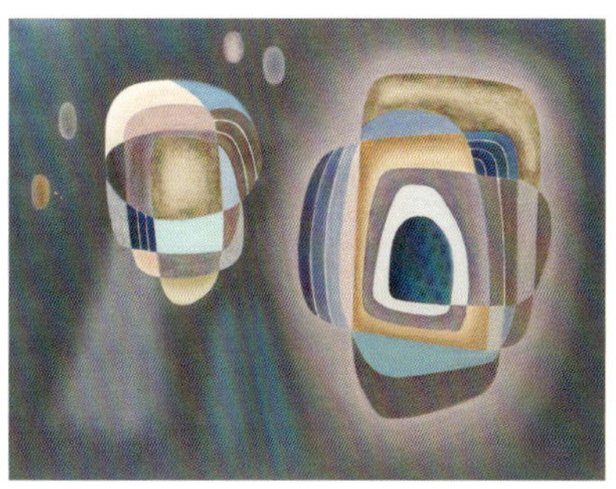

Inscriptions, lower right: "SARU 1976". Verso: "SARU — 1976 — FORME IN SPAŢIU"

(Plate illustration on page 68)

Icon Workshop

91. *Adam and Eve*
Undated, painted glass, 39.4 × 35.6 cm
(15½ × 14 in.), UTT 2017/067

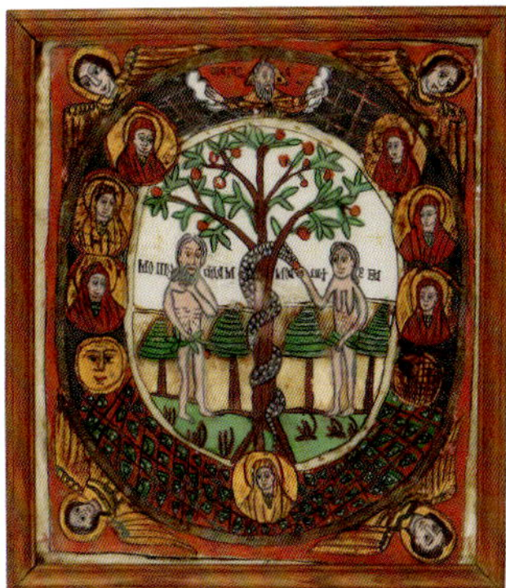

Romania's "icons on glass are my greatest love," Geoffrey wrote to Mariana in 2009. "I find them spiritually very inspiring, painted by and for peasants purely because of their feelings towards God. The simple naïve paintings have a goodness about them that is difficult to describe. It is true that purely as works of art they are not very sophisticated although obviously the skill of the painters improved as time passed, and some of the icons are complicated and semi-professional. The collection that you and Corneliu gave me is a very good one, varied as to the different areas that they came from, varied in terms of subject. . . . Among the 20 I have there is one . . . that I bought from Pacea and two that were gifts from Silvia and Vasile, but the rest are from you and Corneliu."[24]

I found this icon in pieces, wrapped in a towel in a drawer, after Geoffrey's death. It has since been conserved — twice — and remains perilously fragile.

(Plate illustration on page 71)

Endnotes

Beginning in 2006, Geoffrey wrote his letters to Corneliu and Mariana Petrescu, and to Silvia Radu and Vasile Gorduz, on his computer. These can be found online, lightly redacted, at the Tyler Collection Research Repository at the University of Tasmania: tylercollection.omeka.net. His essays on Petrescu, and Corneliu's correspondence with him—on cards with his paintings or collages—are also there, along with much else. The repository catalogues every work in the collection.

Preface

1. Letter to Mariana and Corneliu Petrescu, June 5, 2008.

2. Letter to Mariana, June 13, 2009.

3. Letter to Mariana, May 25, 2009.

4. Letter to Mariana, May 6, 2009.

5. Letter to Mariana, May 5, 2009.

6. Letter to Mariana, November 25, 2009.

7. Letter to Silvia Radu and Vasile Gorduz, January 13, 2006.

8. Letter to Silvia and Vasile, May 23, 2008.

9. Letter to Silvia and Vasile, January 13, 2006. *Dacian Warriors* (utt 2013/532) was indeed heavy; I could not lift it at all.

10. Letter to Mariana and Corneliu, May 23, 2008.

11. Letter to Mariana, May 21, 2009.

12. Letter to Mariana and Corneliu, July 11, 2008.

13. Letter to Mariana and Corneliu, August 16, 2008.

14. Letter to Mariana, May 29, 2009.

15. Letter to Mariana, May 17, 2009.

16. Letter to Mariana and Corneliu, June 12, 2006.

17. Letter to Mariana, May 19, 2009.

Checklist of the Collection

1. Letter to Mariana, July 9, 2010.

2. Letter to the Silvia and Vasile, January 13, 2006.

3. Letter to Mariana and Corneliu, July 13, 2008.

4. Letter to Mariana and Corneliu, July 13, 2008.

5. Sorin Dumitrescu (ed.), *Gorduz: From the Idea to the Apparition; 7 Lessons in Art Making*, Brancoveanu Palace Cultural Centre/Anastasia Foundation, 2010, 51.

6. Letter to Silvia, December 16, 2009.

7. Letter to Mariana, December 18, 2009.

8. Letter to Silvia and Vasile, November 26, 2006.

9. Letter to Silvia, January 7 , 2009.

10. Dan Hăulică in Sorin Dumitrescu (ed.), *Gorduz: From the Idea to the Apparition; 7 Lessons in Art Making*, Brancoveanu Palace Cultural Centre/Anastasia Foundation, 2010, 331.

11. Letter to Silvia, December 16, 2009.

12. Letter to Mariana and Corneliu, August 16, 2008.

13. Letter to Mariana and Corneliu, April 3, 2007.

14. Letter to Mariana and Corneliu, February 9, 2008.

15. Letter to Mariana, July 9, 2010.

16. Letter to Mariana, May 8, 2009.

17. Geoffrey Tyler, "Byzantine Elements in Petrescu's Art," in Tyler Collection Research Repository, University of Tasmania, tylercollection.omeka.net.

18. Letter to Mariana and Corneliu, April 23, 2007.

19. Tyler, "Byzantine Elements in Petrescu's Art," in Tyler Collection Research Repository, University of Tasmania, tylercollection.omeka.net.

20. Tyler, "Byzantine Elements in Petrescu's Art," in Tyler Collection Research Repository, University of Tasmania, tylercollection.omeka.net.

21. Tyler, "Collage in Petrescu's Work," Tyler Collection Research Repository, University of Tasmania, tylercollection.omeka.net.

22. Tyler, "Collage in Petrescu's Work," Tyler Collection Research Repository, University of Tasmania, tylercollection.omeka.net.

23. Letter to Mariana and Corneliu, June 14, 2008.

24. Letter to Mariana, June 6, 2009.

For Further Study

This is virgin territory for scholarship. The Tyler Collection Research Repository (tylercollection.omeka.net) is at present the only complete, accessible source. Just finished, though, is a comprehensive bibliography of Romanian art in the 1970s and 1980s. Available in the Research section of the UTAS Repository, it was compiled by Caterina Preda, Associate Professor at the Department of Political Science, University of Bucharest, under the auspices of the Woodrow Wilson International Center for Scholars. It offers a treasure trove of primary source material.

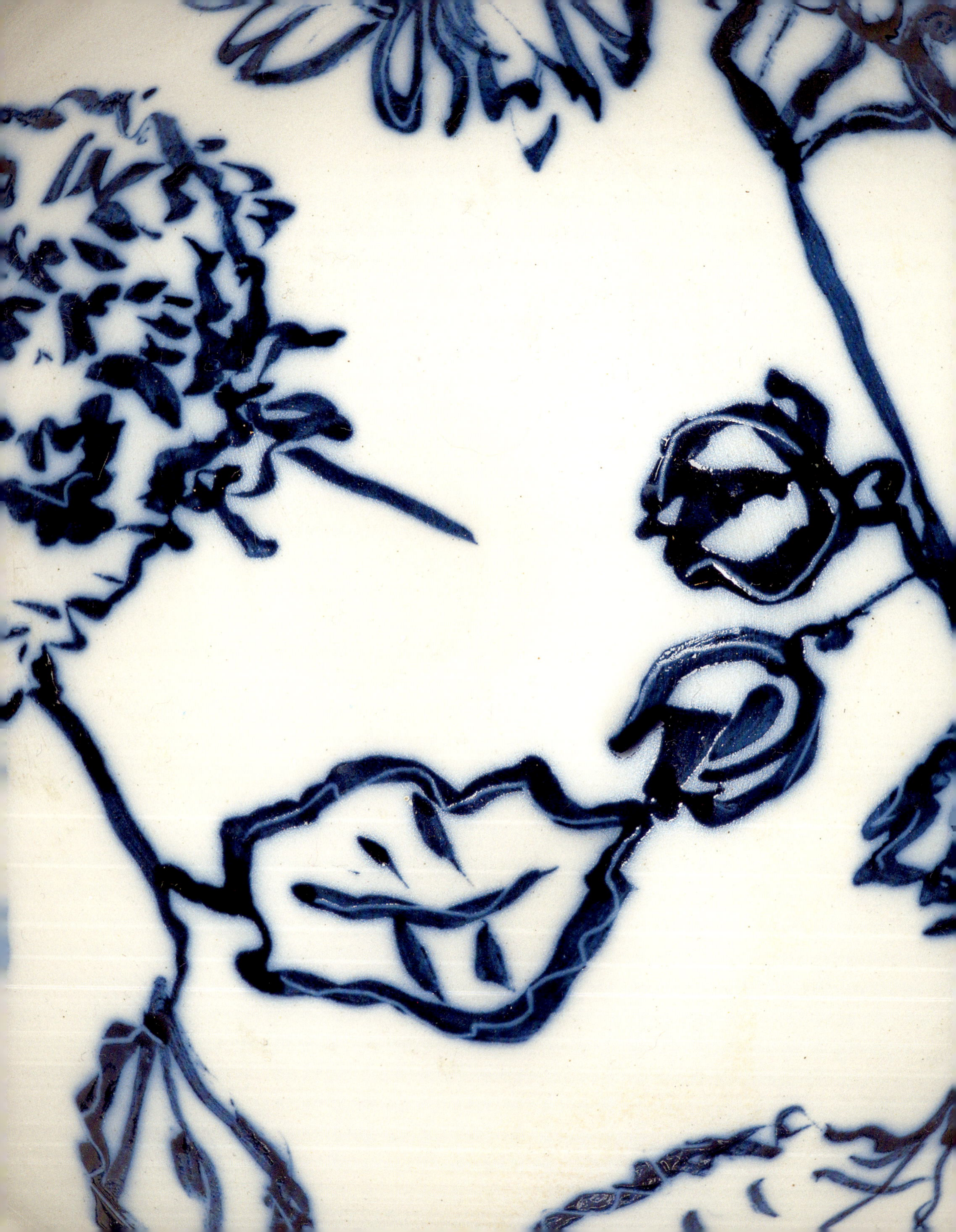

Acknowledgments

Publishing one's own book is a profound adventure. I undertook it wanting to shine a light on the art that I live surrounded by in my house, from a mostly undiscovered period of art history that remains so, even decades after the end of Ceauşescu's repressive dictatorship.

Little did I imagine, back in 1978, how much those evenings of carousing with the Romanian artists in Bucharest would come to mean. These were precious meetings, with creative spirits who had been sealed off from the outside world. Uncovering their art is the reason for this book. I am very grateful indeed to those of you who gave me permission to reproduce your work here. For you others, whom I did try to reach (and perhaps there was a language barrier), I hope that you will nevertheless be pleased with this and that all of you may let me know where I can send you published copies.

To produce *Despite Ceauşescu*, I was fortunate to have the best of the best: Susan Larsen, editor; Margaret Bauer, designer; Lee Ewing, photographer, assisted by art handler Anthony Yannone; and Daniel Frank and his colleagues at Meridian Printing. Leading into this stage were Jay Houston, unframer and reframer of most of the paintings; and Holly Czapski, Krystal Hayden, Arthur Page, and Lori Trusheim, conservators. I thank all of them for their essential, high-quality work.

Nothing would have reached beyond the planning stage without the varied wisdoms of my distinguished advisors and friends (all one and the same): Éduard Andrei, Simon Bevilacqua, Dorian and Daciana Branea, Rhys Conlon, Dennis Deletant, Dru Dowdy, Alan and Lois Fern, Brandon Fortune, Alina Gherasim, Mark Gitenstein, Sam Goodman, Ilie Grigorescu, Daniela Kammrath,

Gregory Lehman, Anamaria Maior, Jeff Malpas, Ann McClellan, Mona Momescu, Stefan Naghiu, Christian Ostermann, Florica and Constantin Pacea, Marc Pachter, Raluca Papagheorghe, Caterina Preda, Silvia Radu, James Rosapepe and his wife Sheilah Kast, Kim Sajet, Radu Stefanescu, and Chris Williams.

Ten years ago, Geoffrey and I visited the University of Tasmania to announce our art collection gift. We were introduced to their Registrar and Curator of the University Fine Art Collection, Rachael Rose. We liked one another instantly. Then and now, through administrative changes at the university, Rachael has been the one constant. Continually creative about finding new ways to explore the collection, she has welcomed me on my annual (until recently) visits to Hobart, developed eye-opening contacts around the world, and arranged trips for both of us, mainly to Romania, where we visited artists or their families — all to enrich our learning about the collection and where it came from. Her brainchild is the online Tyler Collection Research Repository, which includes not only her foundational research (to which this book is indebted) but also useful scholarship from others.

Colophon

This catalogue was designed by Margaret Bauer, who set the text in Milo Pro (which was designed by American type designer Michael Abbink). The book was copyedited by Susan H. Larsen and printed on McCoy Matte (100# text) by Meridian Printing in Rhode Island, with attentive oversight by Daniel Frank. Lee Ewing meticulously photographed the works in the owner's home with the assistance of Anthony Yannone.

About the Author

Frances Tyler headed Publications at the National Portrait Gallery, Smithsonian Institution, for nearly three decades and then became their strategic planning officer. She holds master's degrees from Oxford University (St. Hilda's College, English Language and Literature, 1974) and the Wharton School (Business Administration, 1992). She has lived in Washington, DC, for almost fifty years and shares her late husband's fondness for cats.

Bucharest –
The 3rd of December
1974

Dear Mr. Tyler,

It is long ago since I had no news
from you – and during this period
a lot of things happend... But important
was that my Mother died – also...

I began to peint new paintings
for future exhibitions (when you will
come in Bucharest you'll have the
opportunity to see them.) – Anyhow –
I beg you – to be so kind – and to
help me to have another exhibition there on the Spring 1976 –

For Christmas and New Year –
for you and your wife – the best
wishes of health and happiness
from my wife and me –

Corneliu